AF716884

Money Tree

The Money Printing Machine FX Trading Manual
By Rozen Dube

Company, Authors, and Ownership

Company: Rizen Army

Authors and Ownership:

This publication is the original work of Rozen Dube and is the intellectual property of Rizen Army. All rights are reserved by the authors and the publisher. No portion of this book may be copied, reproduced, or distributed without written consent.

Contact:

- **Email:** rizenarmy@hotmail.com / rozenrizenarmy@gmail.com
- **WhatsApp/Call: +27 75 4736 677**

Together, we rise. Welcome to the RIZEN ARMY.

ISBN

Book Title: *Money Tree (Money Printing Machine FX Trading Manual)*
ISBN: 9781037095634

DISCLAIMER, COPYRIGHTS & LEGAL NOTICES

General Disclaimer

The information presented in this book is intended strictly for **educational and informational purposes**. It does **not** constitute financial, legal, investment, psychological, or professional advice of any kind.

While every effort has been made to ensure the accuracy and reliability of the content, the author and publisher **make no guarantees** and disclaim liability for any loss, injury, or damages arising from the use or misuse of this material. Readers are strongly encouraged to **consult qualified professionals** before acting on any of the content provided.

This publication may contain **strong language or emotionally sensitive material**, and is intended for **mature audiences only**. Reader discretion is advised.

Affiliate Disclosure & Broker Reference

This book may include **promotional or affiliate references** to **XMGlobal**, a forex brokerage platform. These mentions are for **educational and illustrative purposes only**, and do **not** constitute a recommendation, endorsement, or financial guarantee.

The author may earn a commission for referrals made via affiliate links. This does **not affect the integrity** of the educational content provided. Readers are responsible for conducting their own due diligence before choosing any broker or service.

⚠ Risk Warning

Forex trading involves significant risk, including the potential loss of your investment. It is not suitable for all investors. The use of leverage can amplify gains and losses. **Past performance does not guarantee future results.**

The author is **not a licensed financial advisor**, and nothing in this book should be interpreted as professional financial guidance. Always perform independent research or consult a licensed expert before making any trading or investment decisions.

Self-Protection Clause

Any attempt to **distort, misrepresent, defame, weaponize, or exploit** the content of this book for malicious or unlawful purposes will be treated as **intentional misconduct** and may be subject to **civil or criminal legal action**.

Acknowledgements

The author wishes to express sincere gratitude to the following individuals and groups for their unwavering support in the creation of this book:

• **The RIZEN ARMY** — my dedicated team, editors, advisors, and every individual who worked tirelessly behind the scenes. Your belief in this mission made all the difference.

• **Mr. S. Moyo and Mrs. M. Moyo** — my dearest friends and greatest supporters. Your encouragement, wisdom, and investment — both personal and financial — gave me the strength to bring this vision to life.

To all who contributed in ways seen and unseen, thank you. This book is as much yours as it is mine.

Dedication

This book is lovingly dedicated to my beloved son, Mr. O. Tsogang. Your arrival was a divine blessing that lit the same path on which this strategy was born. May your life always reflect the clarity, growth, and courage that inspired these pages.

To every reader seeking to master Forex and rise above limitation — this book is also for you. May it equip you not just with technical tools, but with the mindset to succeed in every battle you face.

TABLE OF CONTENTS

Introduction

Phase 1: Getting Started

Phase 2: The Basics

Phase 3: The Rules

Phase 4: The Strategy

🔤 ABBREVIATIONS

Abbreviation	Meaning
BS	Base Signal
GS	Gape Signal
SL	Stop Loss

Introduction: Where the Roots Go Wrong

Despite all the videos you've watched on YouTube, and despite all the strategies, courses, and so-called "secrets" you've heard, you're still struggling to make consistent profits.

Maybe the YouTubers are wrong.
Maybe they're not telling us the whole truth.
Or maybe — they only know how to speak, not how to teach.

What I do know is this: **something is missing.**

Everyone talks about market direction. They give you entry setups, talk about stop-losses and take-profits, and preach discipline and patience. However, no one talks about **directional probability**. No one shows you how to actually manage your money in a way that builds something sustainable. No one helps you align your **strategy, risk, and psychology** into a complete system that grows with you.

You're given fragments. Moreover, you're expected to build a tree from scattered leaves.

In this manual, I'll Walk you through what you might have been doing wrong — and more importantly, how to fix it. Whether it's your approach to analysis, risk management, or mindset, I'll show you how each part connects to the next. Because **trading isn't just technical — it's personal.**

I believe the **basics of forex only account for about 10%** of your long-term success. Strategy, risk management, and psychology each account for the other 90%. In addition, the deeper truth is: **we all have access to the same 10%.** It's how we apply the remaining 90% that sets us apart.

Here is something most people won't tell you: not all risk management is the same. A fundamental trader who trades high-impact events like NFP or CPI might risk 50% or even 100% of their equity on a single trade. For them, that *is* risk management — and it makes sense *within* their strategy.

That's the point. A trader's **strategy shapes their behaviour**, their emotional responses, and their entire psychology. It's not just about controlling your emotions or setting stop-losses. It's about finding a method that teaches you **how to behave**, how to **risk wisely**, and how to **see the market through your own lens** — not someone else's highlight reel.

In addition, that's why most of the industry feels like a lie.

Some of the loudest voices in trading didn't succeed through skill — they succeeded through luck. Moreover, when luck faded, they pivoted to selling signals, indicators, courses, and memberships. Because if forex truly worked for them, they wouldn't need to monetize your hope.
You don't sell the ladder if you've already climbed it. You keep climbing.

So, before we begin, let's clear the noise.
This isn't another get-rich system.
It's not another patched-up strategy.

It's a foundation — a system rooted in clarity, truth, and growth. It's your seed. Your soil. Your first real step toward growing a **Money Tree** that doesn't just look good — it lasts.

Turn the page. Let's start from the roots.

Phase One: Getting Started

Essential Tools and Resources for Forex Trading

Smartphone/Computer

- **Purpose**: Used for trading, analysis, and staying connected to the market.
- **Definition**: A reliable device that allows you to access your trading platform, monitor markets, and make informed decisions.

Internet

- **Purpose**: To trade successfully, you will need a stable and fast internet connection.
- **Definition**: A good internet connection ensures that your trades are executed smoothly and you stay updated with real-time market movements.

Forex Basics

- **Purpose**: To understand the fundamental concepts of forex trading.
- **Definition**: This manual does not cover the basics of forex; for foundational knowledge, visit YouTube or other educational resources to familiarize yourself with forex trading fundamentals.

Broker & Account

- **Purpose**: To execute trades in the forex market, you need a broker and a trading account.
- **Definition**: A reliable broker like **XMGlobal** offers both standard and micro accounts with competitive spreads.

A Strategy

- **Purpose**: To guide your trading decisions and increase profitability.
- **Definition**: This manual provides a step-by-step strategy to trade and generate consistent profits in forex.

The Test(s)

- **Purpose**: To ensure that you have tested your skills and are ready to trade.
- **Definition**: Before trading study yourself, live- and back-test your strategy in various areas.
  Note: *If you don't have a desktop or tablet, you can skip the back test but still need to complete the other test.*

Sheets

- **Purpose**: To track and improve your trading.
- **Definition**: Various sheets will help organize your trades:
  - Trading Rules
  - Cheat Sheets (Signals)
  - Trading Diary

Tip: *Place the rules and cheat sheets somewhere visible.*

Bank Account & Capital

- **Purpose**: To fund your trading account and manage your forex investments.
- **Definition**: You'll need a bank account that supports forex transactions with **XMGlobal**.
  - **Minimum Capital**: $200 is the minimum required to trade US100Cash with a 0.1 lot size.

Phase Two: The Basics

What is a Strategy?

The term "strategy" is indirectly derived from the Classic and Byzantine Greek word **"strategos"**, which means "general." The original meaning of "strategy" is "order"—**literally the ordering of formations on the battlefield**. In forex, a strategy is a well-thought-out plan of action designed to achieve a long-term or overall goal. It is the art of planning and directing operations and movements in the market to achieve consistent success.

What is Risk Management?

Risk management is an ongoing process of identifying, analyzing, evaluating, and addressing potential loss exposures. It involves monitoring risk control and financial resources to mitigate the adverse effects of loss. These risks can arise from various sources, including financial uncertainties, strategic management errors, accidents, and even natural disasters.

In forex, we use risk management to identify potential problems before they occur—or, in the case of opportunities, to exploit them to our advantage. There are four main types of risk management:

What Does Psychology Mean in Forex?

The word **"psychology"** comes from two Greek terms: **"psyche"** (meaning breath, soul, life, or spirit) and **"logos"** (meaning the study of). In general, psychology refers to the study of the human mind and its functions, particularly how behavior is affected in a specific context.

In forex, psychology refers to the **behavioral aspects of both the market and the trader**. Every currency pair, index, and stock have its own unique characteristics and patterns, which tend to repeat over time. Understanding these patterns and the behavior behind them is crucial for successful trading.

Forex doesn't just teach you how to trade—it also provides lessons that can be applied to real-life situations. Just like in the business world, your grades, innocence, or even professional credentials won't necessarily protect you from financial struggles. So, it's essential to pay attention to the lessons forex teaches, not just in trading, but also in understanding your own psychology and the markets you engage with.

Questions and Answers

- **Have you ever opened a trade but couldn't decide where to place your stop-loss or take-profit?**

- **Are most of your trades moving in your direction only to hit your stop-loss before you can secure a profit?**

- **Why is it that you sometimes hold onto a profitable trade, only to end up closing it at a loss?**

- **Are you cutting your profits short while letting your losses run full?**

Lack of Knowledge:

Winning in forex is not automatic. This means you're most likely to make money when you actually know what you're doing. The wealthy know exactly what they're doing—they've spent time learning and refining their methods. Getting rich is a journey, not a quick fix.

If you're not sure about what you're doing, or if you can't name or describe your strategy clearly, it's time to take a break from trading. Stop testing new strategies, robots, or indicators with your last bit of money. Honestly, the YouTube videos and books I've read didn't work out for me either. It always felt like the market was one step ahead. Maybe all these people are defrauding us, maybe not—I honestly can't tell.

The reason behind your losses is that you don't understand the ins and outs of your strategy. Every strategy has its own unique signals, psychology, and money management rules. In this book, you'll learn how to time your trades, protect your capital, and know when to exit. I'll share my backtesting results (history) and offer tests to help you see if you truly understand the strategy.

Bear with me—the only way to succeed is by being rational. This means using logic and being realistic. No shortcuts, just hard work. It's nearly impossible to trade without emotions. If I tell you not to trade when you're angry or sad, you'll probably still trade. Once you get started, it's hard to stop.

So, what's the best solution if you're feeling emotional? Buy a robot, have someone manage the trades for you, or read this book thoroughly. Learn all the ins and outs of this powerful strategy, and you're more likely to see consistent profits.

Signs of Lack of Knowledge:

- You can't explain your strategy in detail, including its origin, performance, and how you plan to approach it for your benefit.

- Every strategy should have rules. If yours doesn't, you're just gambling. These rules should not only cover the winning side, but also how to handle losses.

- You don't know when or where to enter a trade.

- You struggle to accept losses (feeling guilty) or recognize your mistakes.

- You're too emotional—this is one of the biggest signs that you don't know what you're doing (we all turn to God, our ancestors, or alcohol when things go wrong).

Solution(s):

This book is a step-by-step manual designed to show you what to do to get rich through forex. If you feel like you've been studying incomplete or incorrect strategies, then this book is exactly what you need.

Lack of Understanding:

You may read this entire book, feel confident, and think, "Wow, I've got this!"—and then *boom*, blow your account.

Knowledge is one of the most important aspects of this manual. With the right knowledge, you'll be able to tell if the market is likely to sell or buy. Yes, you can understand everything in this manual and still fail to apply it properly. Many traders know about support and resistance, market sessions, FVGs (Fair Value Gaps), and all these other incredible concepts, but they still fail to apply them effectively. Even if they can apply the knowledge, they might not know when to exit or how to avoid traps.

The solution to this problem is simple: **16 weeks of live testing**. The only way to truly measure your understanding is by testing yourself in real-time.

Experience beats knowledge. I will also explain how to trade in difficult zones and how to handle moments when you don't feel 100% confident.

Signs of Lack of Understanding:

- Changing rules or plans without a clear reason.
- Making the same mistakes over and over, only realizing it later (e.g., the market hunts your stop loss and then moves in your direction).
- Regretting closing your order too early.
- Trading without a clear plan.
- Feeling impatient and lacking confidence.
- Praying for your trades to go in the right direction.

Solution(s):

To truly understand and master your strategy, you need to study it through both live testing and back testing. Pay attention to the similarities you find in both types of testing. Track the average return and loss, and use statistical analysis (math) to evaluate your strategy. Then, create your own plan based on this data.

Confusion:

Most traders did not receive proper training when they first started with forex. As a result, there's a lot of unnecessary information floating around with no real purpose.

In this manual, I'd like to ask you not to apply what you've learned from the past, even if it once worked for you. Avoid applying too many things at once, as this will lead to confusion. You are not an expert, and you will never be—no one is all-knowing. To minimize confusion, challenge your strategy by examining its worst-case scenarios: high liquidities, biggest losses, drawdowns, average losses, rough zones, and ranging periods. Keep redoing the tests repeatedly. By doing so, you'll find ways to eliminate confusion.

This will also teach you how to trade through rough zones and handle aggressive market movements.

Do not combine this strategy with other methods you know. As we both know, too much information leads to confusion, especially when you start mixing in trend lines or small-time frames. These minor techniques should be avoided.

Signs of Confusion:

- One moment you're buying, the next you're selling.
- Today, you're following this strategy; tomorrow, you're using Telegram signals or indicators.
- Becoming anxious about your positions and trying to "fix" them as if something is wrong.
- Disorder and over-complicating things.

Solution(s):

Every successful person is known for focusing on one thing. I'm not saying you should quit your job or drop out of school to focus solely on forex. What I am saying is: **don't combine my strategy with others'** or use multiple strategies that aren't working. Grow up, man—those other strategies failed before. Now pay attention: **One secret code is all it takes to change everything.**

Environment(s):

Numerous studies have shown that our environment has a significant impact on our character and behavior. My father was born here, and I can point to where his tombstone lies. My mother knows every corner of this city.

I live right next to a tavern, and across from me is a primary school. Every day, the loudspeakers buzz until 3 AM, and at 7 AM, the schoolchildren scream as if they're rushing with the wind, while the siren blares at 8 AM. It's a constant source of torment. If it's not the kids on weekdays, it's the church drums on the weekends. I used to be a genius in high school, and I always thought I could study in noisy environments. Well, I'm older now. Focus requires silence, and my house can't offer that.

Back in the day, music used to hit differently. We were carefree, dancing all night, and sleep came easily. Being a man used to mean having attractive girls around, and for girls, it was about dating the most wanted guy in town. It was all about clothes, style, and alcohol. Of course, some men never grow up, and some can't escape that lifestyle. They remain man-children, and I don't blame them. The chances of getting rich are slim. Not all of us have special talents or the connections, nor can we work over 40 hours a week.

But those days are over. The rich keep getting richer, and the poor stay poor. I'm just in the wrong place, and it's not my fault. I want a better life for my family, and that's why I chose to write this manual to help you escape. I'm not happy with where I live now—it's not home, it's just where I grew up. I won't die here. I will escape. I won't stay here when I get rich because rich people don't stay here. I'm going to surround myself with the rich.

Wall Street isn't built in a small village where poverty is the norm. You may even get arrested if you're found poor in such places. When I get rich, I'll stay far away from poverty. But I'm not leaving you alone—this book will be your weapon, just as it has been mine.

Signs of Environmental Problems:

- **Isolation:** People tend to isolate themselves from others or from nature when they don't feel comfortable in their environment. This can lead to depression, loneliness, and ultimately unrealistic goals. Try blending in—there's always someone who shares your character and goals. Stop obsessing over money. Seek adventure, not happiness.
- **Tiredness:** Feeling drained, having poor hygiene, and lacking the energy or appetite to work are all signs of an unhealthy environment.

Solution(s):

Don't get lost in the oblivion. It's not the end of the world. Forex can't be all that you do. Find a team, make friends, and reconnect with your family. You will escape this environment when the time is right. Stay clean, stay grounded, and be content even when things aren't perfect. If the environment is draining you, try working out or going to the gym to clear your mind and regain your energy.

Surrounding and Infections:

It is nearly impossible to be far more different from your surroundings. I'm talking about your friends, partners, and family.

Each one of us carries energy—either negative or positive. If your friends lack ambition, they will keep you busy doing nothing, distracting you from your goals. On the other hand, if you're a successful trader, they will likely ask for money from you constantly. If you're struggling as a trader, they may start saying negative things about your trading, which could lead to doubt, anger, or even revenge.

You can't afford to be stressed by things you can't control. While we don't choose our family, we can choose who we draw close to and who we love from a distance. When it comes to friends and partners, choose wisely. This will free you from self-sabotage. Ask your friends to help you avoid making mistakes, if they can. Talk to them about what you intend to do with your profits. **#What is your money for?** Ask yourself this question to avoid overspending or chasing unrealistic goals.

If you continue making mistakes and realize you weren't thinking clearly when making decisions, take a step back. Self-introspection is key. Understand what might be affecting your judgment. To make clear, focused decisions, you need a clear mindset, patience, and focus. It's healthier to be with someone who doesn't demand much, understands you, and supports you. This will help you stay grounded and stop trying to get rich overnight.

A toxic partner can lead to impatience and a lack of focus. A toxic relationship doesn't necessarily mean the other person is the problem—it might be you. Staying in a toxic relationship can lead to stress, which, in turn, can cause issues like sexual dysfunction, alcohol or drug abuse, anger problems, insecurity, and peer pressure. Your family may also doubt you or oppose your journey if you're not yet profitable—especially if you've misused their money in the past.

Honestly, they're right to be cautious. You could be wasting time and their finances. It's better to learn forex properly before investing and managing your capital wisely, especially if you're new. If you want to involve them, make sure they're supportive and hold you accountable.

Don't force them to believe in you or support you. Remember, they're your family and friends—not your employees.

Signs of Bad Surroundings and Infections:

- **Being Judgmental:** Everything we know about humans has been taught by other humans. No one truly understands how we operate. So, if you feel like you're unique, don't go too far trying to force others to be like you.

- **Mood Swings:** Silent treatment, ignorance, overdoing house chores, or unnecessary cleaning are all examples of mood swings. If you've been blowing accounts and only realize it after the fact, you were likely irritated by your surroundings at the time.

- One of my family members once told me that this forex thing of mine would never work. It wasn't just her—many people around us doubt what we do. Even if they don't say it outright, you can feel it in their actions or see it in their eyes. "This forex thing is just nonsense," they think. They're pushing their own dreams on us. We all have our differences. Don't seek revenge on the market, and don't try to prove them wrong.

- **Not Caring:** Maybe you're just crying for attention. Maybe your partner left you, or something else is bothering you. Whatever it is, stop and think about your future. Don't trade recklessly when you're upset, because sooner or later, you'll regret it. Focus on being independent and don't tie yourself to materialistic things.

- **Drug and Alcohol Abuse:** Maybe you saw someone who's doing well in forex, but they're always posting videos popping champagne. Remember, you're not them, and you don't know their true motives. If they're overindulging, they may be living a lifestyle that won't last long. Worse yet, you may be trying to emulate them, thinking that's the key to success, but their success may be sponsored by someone else or part of a strategy to distract you. If getting rich means dying young, then it's time to rethink things. This book will guide you to wealth without compromising your spirit, body, or soul. Ignore the noise and focus on mastering the skill.

- **Relationships in Your Twenties:** Relationships aren't easy, especially in your twenties. Not everything is about them. Stop trying to please someone at the cost of your well-being. Don't run out of money just trying to keep up with the demands of takers around you. I'm no expert on relationships, but it's important to be judicious with yourself and your resources.

Solution(s):

Stay away from the unlucky and the unhappy. Sometimes, the unlucky bring misery to themselves. If you wish to help a friend or family member, don't rush into it—first, learn the laws of seduction and manipulation, because people only listen to what they want to hear. For now, focus on yourself. Not everything is about them. Stop trying to please others.

Situations:

Yes, you guessed it right—this is where many of our ambitious brothers and sisters lose their way. **Situations are not permanent**, but because of the fear of the unknown, we often rush into decisions driven by our circumstances.

I've been there myself, in debt, and maybe I still owe some people. When I first discovered this strategy, I was working as a mathematics tutor. Tutoring paid well for some, but not for me, as many of my clients took advantage of me being a foreigner. I completed my high school education in South Africa, and later, I struggled to continue my studies because I lacked the financial means. A lot of visas and money were required, and on top of that, there were no bursaries for foreigners.

In the same month that I came up with this strategy, I found out that I was going to be a father. A 19-year-old girl was pregnant with my child, and this book is dedicated to him. Yes, I had a responsibility. At that time, I couldn't even get a job because my passport didn't have a work permit. Plus, with the high unemployment rate in South Africa, even the "green beans" (new recruits) were employed to send us back home. Most foreigners lost their jobs that year.

The only way I could support my family was through forex trading. You may find yourself in a similar—or even worse—situation.

But **do not fall into the trap** of going into debt trying to make money. I regret that decision. **Do not rush things.** The best way to avoid landing in a situation like mine is to understand that forex is not the source of your problems—it's your solution.

Therefore, be **judicious with yourself**. Reward yourself each time you achieve a goal, no matter how small. Small steps lead to huge success.

Signs of This Virus:

- **Rushing leads to crushing**: Take your time. Read, test, and then act. There's no need to hurry; the market will always be there.
- **Giving up, loss of appetite, and living in dirty or unclean environments**: Where is your self-love? Did it die when you were a teenager? Take care of yourself, both mentally and physically, to keep your focus sharp.

Solution(s):

Don't let success go to your head. Never let failure gets to your heart.

Forex trading is a journey, not a race. Your emotional stability, patience, and persistence are the keys to unlocking long-term success. When you take your time, learn, and approach things carefully, you'll be able to avoid the pitfalls that others often fall into.

YOU:

Yes, **you**—you are the problem. You don't have a clear plan to make money. You lack the faith and tenacity needed to succeed. And most importantly, you treat your body poorly: you eat badly, work excessively, and sleep like a dog.

Every rich person knows this: **money is not what makes you rich.** Even if you master this strategy and start making money, you might find yourself broke again and again. The issue is not about making money—it's about having the right character to handle it. Give money to a thief, and they will steal more. Give money to a killer, and they will kill more. The biggest problem is not the challenges you face—it's **you.**

You are your biggest problem.

In this manual, I will give you the plans and strategies for trading, but if you're disorganized, you'll still risk your money. **Being organized gives you a one-hour head start.** Stay organized, and the money will come.

After I discovered this strategy, I still lost money. I blew my account more than three times. The problem wasn't the market, nor the strategy—it was **me**. I was unorganized. There was too much disorder in my approach, which led to another 12 months of being broke.

With **great money** (or power, or influence) comes **great responsibility**. Every penny you waste now will turn into a regret later. Therefore, be **organized**, develop a strong mindset, and take responsibility.

Signs That You Are Wrong:

- **Disorder**: Lack of structure or routine.
- **Lying**: Deceiving yourself or others.
- **Laziness**: Not putting in the necessary effort.
- **Tiredness**: Burnout or exhaustion from working incorrectly.
- **Blaming others or circumstances**: Avoiding accountability.
- **Praying for the market**: Hoping for luck instead of putting in the work.
- **Stressing out**: Allowing anxiety and worry to take over.
- **Multi-tasking**: Spreading yourself too thin and losing focus.
- **Being tyrannical**: Controlling everything out of fear or insecurity.

Solution(s):

Take action. I've put together some work for you, but **don't start trading without doing the groundwork**. Test yourself and identify the weaknesses in your character. Work on fixing those first.

Be honest with yourself about where you're falling short, and do the work to improve. Your success is not just about what you know—it's about who you are. Stay organized, stay disciplined, and take responsibility for your actions.

Capital:

Capital refers to the resources you use to build, run, or grow a business. In the context of trading, it's not just the money you use to trade, but also includes things like equipment, internet, a dedicated workspace, and more.

Without sufficient capital, **do not attempt to trade**—unless you have a solid plan to approach the market. If you're low on capital, then focus on securing a stable income first—get a 9-to-5 job, save up, and return to trading once you have enough funds. Alternatively, you can look for investors or consider bootstrapping. **Practice every day** to prepare yourself for when the time is right.

Be cautious about getting investors. If you promise more than you can deliver, you could end up in trouble. Always be honest and transparent in your dealings.

You can also open a joint trading account with others, but make sure they're using the same strategy and agree on the terms of the partnership. **Clarity and mutual understanding are key** when it comes to collaborating.

Signs of Insufficient Capital:

- **Being too emotional**: Allowing fear or excitement to control your decisions.
- **Breaking the rules**: Taking excessive risks because you're desperate for profits.
- **Thinking forex is only about making money**: Forgetting that risk management and discipline are just as important.
- **Being greedy**: Trying to earn big returns too quickly, which often leads to failure.
- **Anger towards the market**: Frustration due to lack of funds can lead to poor decisions.

Solution(s):

- **Get what's necessary**: Make sure you have the capital, or find a way to get it.
- **Get an investor**: If you choose this route, be honest and clear about expectations.
- **Open a joint account**: Partner with others who are on the same page about trading strategies.
- **Risk what you have with precaution**: Only trade with what you can afford to lose. Avoid gambling with your last savings.

MAJOR SOLUTION: Love What You Do

The core solution to all the challenges you face in trading comes down to one word: **love**. Let me explain.

Back in 2015, when I was in grade 8, I was the top mathematics student. Even today, this is a rare feat—one that many still struggle to achieve globally. At that time, I realized something important: **you can only master something if you truly fall in love with it**. It's not just about hard work, it's about passion.

You might ask yourself, **"Do I love forex trading, or am I just doing it for the money?"** If your answer is the latter, then unfortunately, you'll struggle to succeed in this game. **Love** is the key to unlocking greatness. **If you do not love forex trading**, you will not make it—not because you don't have the skills or knowledge, but because your mindset will be focused on money, not the craft.

It seems like 90% of traders are motivated by the desire to make money, not by the love of the game. This is often because of how forex trading is presented—most people see it as a quick path to wealth. But to master it, you need to fall in love with the process.

Why Hard Work Isn't the Primary Factor

You've probably heard the saying, **"To achieve greatness, you need to work hard."** This is true, but it depends on the context. Yes, if you're building a house or running a factory, hard work is essential. But **forex trading is not the same**.

For example, I spend just a few seconds analyzing my trades every 4 hours. That's less than an hour a day spent on analysis.

In my view, trading is not about working tirelessly for hours.

If you approach trading with the mindset that you need to work yourself into the ground, you'll end up overcomplicating things. You might feel like every time you want to trade; you need to spend hours analyzing the market. That's a recipe for burnout, and it leads to more mistakes.

This is why I don't recommend tools like **Trading View**—they're too entertaining and packed with so many tools and indicators that they can easily distract you. You don't need all of that.

Why You Should Fall in Love with Forex Trading

Imagine this: You've been working hard at math, spending countless hours solving problems, and still, you fail the test. **That's what happened to me**. I spent years watching YouTube videos, attending free seminars, drawing lines on charts, downloading indicators from Telegram... sound familiar?

I was doing all of this to avoid feeling guilty about my failure. **I lost time, money, and tools** because I was focused on the wrong thing—just making money. Maybe you've been in the same place, trying everything, but still not seeing the results you hoped for.

When you love something, you don't just work at it—you **become obsessed** with it. You study it deeply, pay attention to the smallest details, and eventually, it becomes second nature. It's like the subject sticks with you. You even dream about it. **That's when you start truly learning and mastering a skill**.

If you want to get good at math, you first have to fall in love with it. The same applies to forex trading. **When you truly love forex trading**, you won't just focus on making money. Instead, you'll focus on mastering the skill, improving every day, and becoming better at understanding the market.

When you shift your focus from money to **love and mastery**, **the pressure eases**. Patience becomes your ally, and success will follow naturally.

Conclusion: Focus on Mastery, Not Money

In the end, the most important thing you can do is **fall in love with forex trading**. When you develop a passion for it, the money will follow. However, more importantly, you will develop the skills and patience necessary to sustain long-term success.

So, stop chasing quick profits and start learning to enjoy the process. Love the art of trading, and it will make the journey much more rewarding.

Phase Three: The Rules

1. Time Intervals (Alarms)

- Trade during the following time intervals: **0:00, 04:00, 08:00, 12:00, 16:00, and 20:00** from Monday to Friday (Pretoria, Harare **GTM +02:00**). These intervals are based on the market sessions within a 4-hour timeframe and are subject to change according to market conditions and location.

- The alternative alarm (for times when the market is closed during the week) is usually one hour away/before from the original alarm time.

- **Start trading on Monday**, unless your initial orders didn't turn a profit, in which case you may start at any time after.

- Always trade on the **4-hour timeframe** for consistency and precision.

- **Flexibility**: With this strategy, you can trade during work or school hours without interference, as it is designed to fit your schedule. Analyzing take few seconds for professionals.

2. Overlapping Orders & Pending Trades

- Some trades may carry over to the next week due to lack of manual exits.
- **Do not enter a trade in the middle of a pending order** if the trade has already moved in the intended direction (in profit).
- If the order has not yet moved in the intended direction, you may enter, but **ensure a proper stop loss is in place**.
- This rule is designed to help you **avoid missing profitable trades** while reducing the risk of collecting losing trades.

3. Stay Out After a Trade

- After placing a long or short position, **stay out of the market for the next 4 hours**.
- This rule is in place to help **avoid emotional trading** and give the market time to develop without impulsive decisions.

---

4. Account Type

- This strategy is best implemented on **XMGlobal broker**, specifically using a spread account type (standard or micro).

---

5. Required Capital for Trading

- You will need a minimum of **$890** to trade with **0.1 lot size** on each cash index.
- For trading the three indexes (**US100Cash, US30Cash, Ger40Cash**), ensure you have sufficient equity:
    - You may start with $200, trading US100cash only.

---

6. Strategy for Entry

- Use one of the signals provided in this manual to enter your orders. Stick to the strategy's rules and **do not deviate**. This manual consists of twelve base signals and four gape signals.

7. No Consecutive Long/Short Orders

- **Do not place long and short orders consecutively**. For example:
    - Go **long after a short signal**.
    - Go **short after a long signal**.
- Avoid entering a second position on the same trade direction (i.e., no consecutive long or short orders).
- Focus on **reversals** unless specifically instructed otherwise by the strategy.

---

8. 4-Hour Period Only

- This strategy **only works on the 4-hour timeframe**.

- **Do not try to use it on other timeframes or indexes** unless it works perfectly for you.

- **Avoid looking for "perfect" entries** on minor timeframes (like 1-hour or 15-minutes), as this can lead to impulsive decisions, overtrading, and gambling behaviors.

9. Stop Loss Rules

- Set your **stop loss** according to the strategy:
  - If your stop loss is **too wide (e.g., 70,000 points or more), adjust it to around 30,000 points**.
  - If your stop loss is **too tight (e.g., 2,000 points)**, **increase it to 4,000 points**.
- **Do not adjust stop losses** on pending orders. These should remain fixed until either manual exit or the stop loss is hit. Adjusting stop losses after the order is placed is a risky practice that does not have a clear plan or probability.

10. Manual Exits

- **Use manual exits to close your trades**.
  - For example, close a **bullish order** to enter a short position and vice versa for a **bearish order**.
- **Avoid taking second buy/sell orders** that are close to the reversal point, as these orders might invalidate the setup.
- You may **move stop loss** to the **pending signal entry level** for **automation**.
- Manual exits are crucial because they help you:
  - Memorize chart patterns.
  - Develop your **skill in reading the market** and understanding the strategy's nuances.
  - Control emotional reactions and stay focused on your plan.

Phase Four: The Strategy

Valid and Invalid Entries: Understanding Reversals and Avoiding Traps

In this strategy, the focus is on ***reversal entries****, not on chasing consecutive signals. Here's how to interpret and act on valid and invalid signals:*

1. Valid Entries: Reversals Only

- **Reversal signals** are the most reliable entries. You should only take a **sell signal if your previous signal was a buy**, and vice versa.
- A **reversal** means the market is likely to change direction after a previous trend. This is where the **true opportunity lies**.

  For example:

  - If your previous signal was a **buy**, and a sell signal appears, **this is a valid entry**.
  - If your previous signal was a **sell**, and a buy signal appears, **this is a valid entry**.
- **Look for confirmation** that the new signal opposes the previous one. If they are opposing, it's a strong indication of a reversal.

2. Invalid Entries: Continuous Signals

- **Do not take consecutive signals** in the same direction. Repeating the same signal without a reversal can be a **trap** designed for the greedy trader.

  For example:
  - If you receive a **buy signal**, and then another **buys signal** follows immediately, **do not trade** it.
  - Similarly, if you get a **sell signal** followed by another **sell signal**, this is likely an unreliable setup.
- **Why?** These consecutive signals are usually **false traps** designed to mislead traders into thinking the trend will continue indefinitely, leading to impulsive and emotional decisions.
- "**Unless** the first signal didn't trigger or the price hasn't moved in the desired direction, you should not enter. If you missed the initial signal under those conditions, you may still enter. However, if you already entered on the first signal, you should ignore any subsequent signals.

---

3. Stop Hunts & Long Candles

- **Stop Hunts** or **long candles** can sometimes invalidate the reversal signals. This market movements often occur to "hunt" stop losses or create sudden volatility that may mislead traders into taking wrong positions.
  - If you see a **long candle** or a **stop hunt**, be cautious. Even though the previous signal may have been a valid reversal, this new movement can be a **false breakout**. In such cases, it is essential to **analyze the market context** before taking the trade.

---

4. Analyzing Signals:

- **Step 1**: Before considering any new signal, **analyze the previous signal**.
- **Step 2**: Ask yourself:
    - Does the new signal oppose the previous one? If yes, **this could be a reversal** and a valid entry.
    - Does the new signal follow the same direction as the previous one? **Avoid taking this trade**, as it may lead to overtrading and unnecessary losses.
    - "Only enter if the first signal didn't trigger or the price hasn't moved in the desired direction. In that case, you may enter if you missed the initial signal. However, if you already entered on the first signal, you can ignore any subsequent signals."
- **Remember**: A true **reversal** is what you seek, not a continuous move in the same direction. Patience and discipline are key when waiting for a reversal setup.

THE STRATEGY

✓ Practical Use

BUY SIGNAL

- exit sell, in profit
- pending BUY
- order trigged, then sl hit due to stop hunt
- re-enter BUY

SELL SIGNAL

- SL moved to pending SELL level
- order didn't trigger in 24hrs
- manual delete order
- move sl (BUY) to its original level

SELL SIGNAL

- exit buy, in profit
- enter SELL

BUY SIGNAL

- close sell, in loss
- enter BUY
- cureent BUY hits SL

SELL SIGNAL

- enter SELL

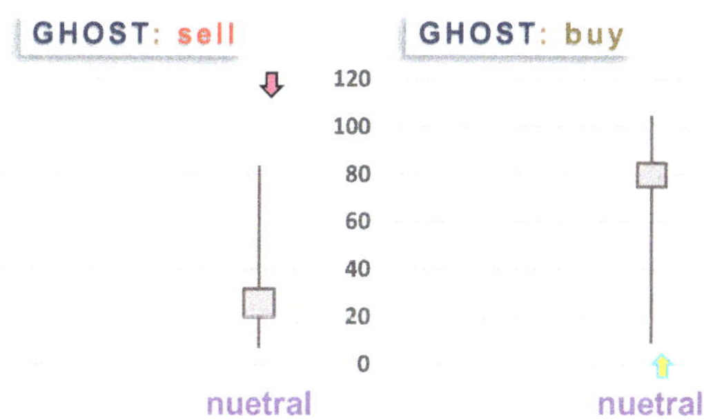

Trade Recovery Protocol

a) You opened a position based on one of the eleven base signals.
b) The trade was stopped out due to a stop hunt — price hit your stop loss, then quickly reversed.
c) As soon as the candlestick closes, re-enter the trade immediately.
d) Set your new stop loss just beyond the opposite end of the candle that triggered your re-entry.

BS4 → Delta

Definition

Base Signal Number Four, also known as **“The Three Candles”** or **“Delta”**, is a reversal pattern built on three consecutive candles that indicate a shift in market direction. This pattern often forms at the end of a trend and marks the exhaustion point through trap behavior. The **middle candle sets the trap**, and the final candle confirms the reversal, signaling the entry using stop orders.

◆ Signal Logic

This signal thrives on reversal logic, where a shift in sentiment happens subtly over three candles:

1. **Candle ①:** Follows the direction of the prevailing trend.

2. **Candle ②:** Opposes the trend, creating a potential **trap low or high**.
3. **Candle ③:** Aligns with Candle ②, confirming the shift in direction.

The second candle is always the **lowest or highest point** of the three, setting up the trap. A **stop order** is placed 1200 points beyond the high/low of the confirming candle (Candle ③).

◆ Signal Criteria

BUY Reversal (After Downtrend):

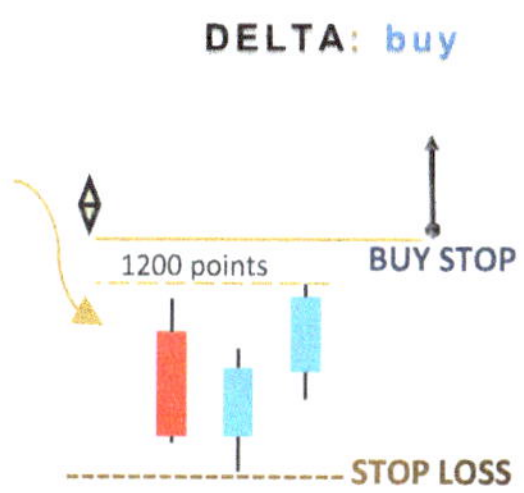

- Candle ①: Bearish (continuing the downtrend).
- Candle ②: Bullish (lowest low of the three).
- Candle ③: Bullish again (confirmation).
- Candle③ should close higher than Candle②.
- Place a BUY STOP 1200 points above the high of Candle ③.
- Stop Loss: on the low of Candle ②.

SELL Reversal (After Uptrend):

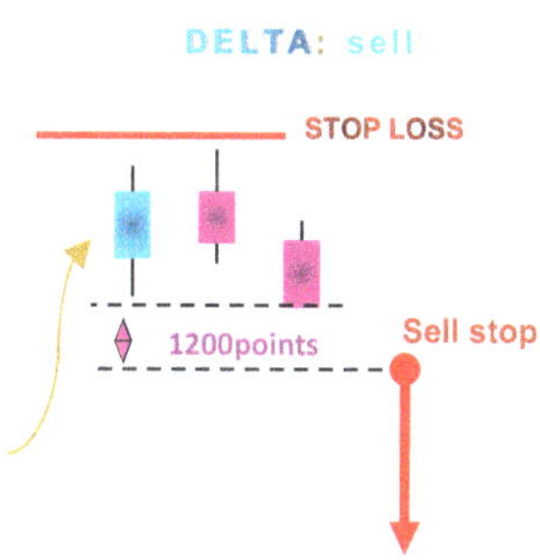

- Candle ①: Bullish (continuing the uptrend).
- Candle ②: Bearish (highest of the three).
- Candle ③: Bearish again (confirmation).
- Candle ③ should close lower than Candle②.
- Place a SELL STOP 1200 points below the low of Candle ③.
- Stop Loss: on the high of Candle ②.

◆ **Weak Signals**

• If all three candles are small or have no conviction.
• When the second candle doesn't clearly make a new high/low.
• Structure forms in the middle of a choppy range or consolidation.
• The reversal does not align with a larger market context or key level.

◆ **Entry & Stop Loss Strategy**

• Use **stop orders only**.
• Entry is placed **1200 points** beyond Candle ③'s high (buy) or low (sell).
• **Stop Loss** is placed on the opposite side of Candle ②.
• If the setup is not triggered within 4 hours, the order should be canceled.

◆ **Conditions to Confirm the Signal**

• A clear **preceding trend** must be present.
• The second candle must **indicate a reversal.**
• The third candle must show **strong confirmation** in the opposite direction.

◆ **Invalid Signals**

• If Candle ② is not the dominant of the three.
• If Candle ③ doesn't close convincingly in the direction of reversal.

◆ Order Management

• Cancel the pending order if not triggered within **4hours**.
• Do not stack with conflicting signals—wait for structure reset.
• Once the trade moves in your favor, do not move SL to breakeven after the first impulse candle.

BS5 → The Star

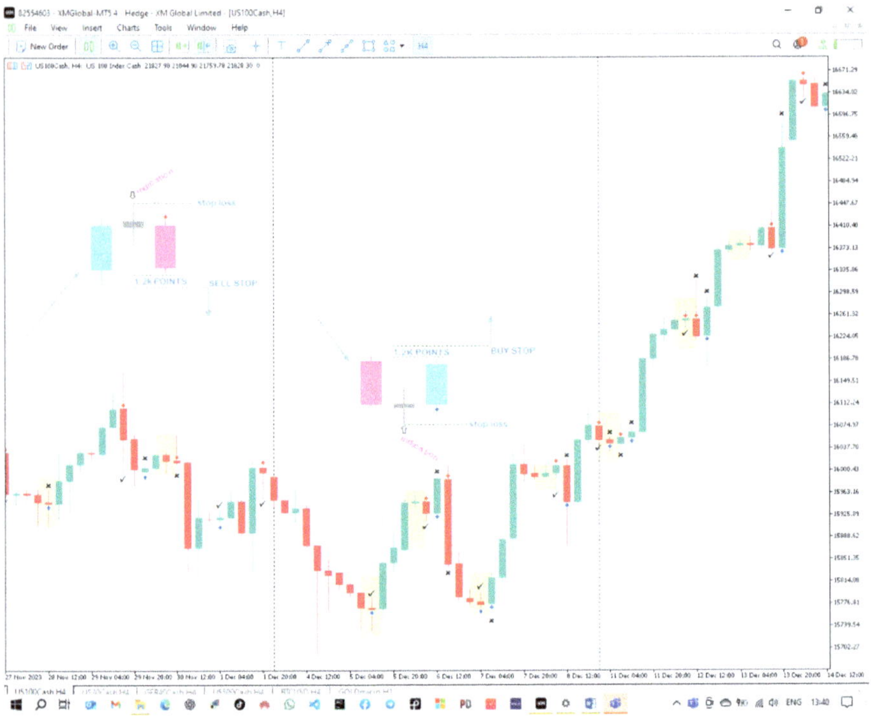

Definition

Base Signal Number Five is a three-candle reversal pattern known as *The Star*. It forms after a strong directional move and signals exhaustion in momentum. This pattern focuses on the psychological pause between aggressive buyers and sellers, where the middle candle—known as the "star"—represents indecision and signals a likely reversal. The signal is recognized by a visually distinct structure with a dominant middle wick (or a doji-style body), surrounded by two nearly equal candles in size and volume.

◈ Signal Logic

The pattern consists of three candles:

1. **Candle ①:** Strong directional candle aligned with the prevailing trend.
2. **Candle ② (The Star):** Neutral candle, typically with no body or very small body, must have a long wick—downward or upward, sometimes equivalent wicks.
3. **Candle ③:** Opposite-direction candle, nearly equal in size to Candle ①, confirming the reversal.

This structure suggests a momentum pause, a liquidity grab, and a shift in market direction.

◈ Signal Criteria

BUY Reversal (After Downtrend):

- Candle ①: Bearish.
- Candle ②: Neutral or small-bodied candle, yet dominant (can be bullish or bearish).
- Candle ③: Bullish and nearly equal in size to Candle ①.
- Place a BUY STOP 1200 points above the high of Candle ③.
- Stop Loss: on the low of Candle ②.

SELL Reversal (After Uptrend):

- Candle ①: Bullish.
- Candle ②: Neutral or small-bodied candle, yet dominant (can be bullish or bearish).
- Candle ③: Bearish and nearly equal in size to Candle ①.
- Place a SELL STOP 1200 points below the low of Candle ③.
- Stop Loss: on the high of Candle ②.

◆ Weak Signals

- Candle ② lacks dominance.
- Candles ① and ③ differ significantly in size or momentum.
- Appears during low volume or flat consolidation.
- The signal occurs without a strong trend preceding it.

◆ Entry & Stop Loss Strategy

- **Always use stop orders.**
- Entry: 1200 points past the breakout side of Candle ③ (high for BUY, low for SELL).
- SL: on the low for a buy and high for a sell of Candle ②.
- If the order isn't triggered within 4hours, **cancel** the setup.

◆ Conditions to Confirm the Signal

- Appears at the end of a trend (up or down).
- Candle ② shows a clear exhaustion wick (grabbing stops/liquidity).
- Price is reacting from a key level (supply/demand, support/resistance).

◆ Invalid Signals

- Candle ② has no dominance or appears an FVG.
- Candle ③ closes weak or is too small to confirm momentum.

◆ Order Management

- Cancel any pending order if not triggered in 4 hours.
- If a new valid signal appears, **prioritize the latest**.

🔍 Be Observant

- Candle ② is key—it should pause or wick into liquidity.
- Look for equal-sized candles on either side for clean symmetry.
- Confirm location: key zones, after sharp trends.
- The Star often appears at turning points when momentum flips.

BS6 → Inside Reversal

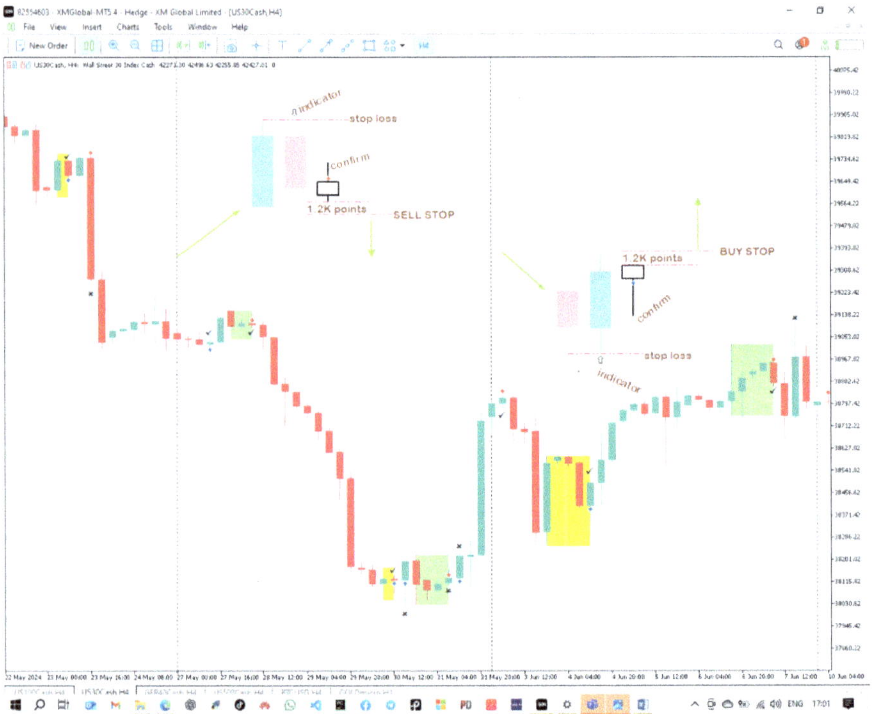

Definition

Base Signal Number Six called inside reversal is a **three-candle reversal trap** that forms at the **end of a trend**, designed to catch liquidity before a major price reversal. It focuses on **market structure exhaustion**, where momentum fades and traps are set using false breakouts and inside bars. The pattern is built to identify when smart money is likely to reverse the market after faking a continuation.

◆ Signal Logic

After a strong trend (up or down), the market prints a three-candle pattern:

1. **Candle ①**: Strong in the direction of the trend (momentum).
2. **Candle ②**: Opposite to the trend—a potential fake reversal begins.
3. **Candle ③**: Fully contained inside Candle ②, showing compression, indecision, and the final trap.

Once the third candle forms, the reversal setup is complete. A **stop order** is placed to catch the breakout **against** the prior trend, confirming the reversal move.

◈ Signal Criteria

SELL Reversal (After Uptrend):

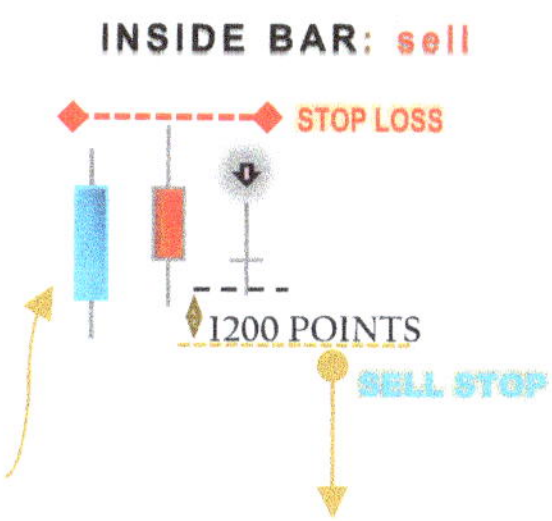

a) Candle ①: Bullish (momentum).
b) Candle ②: Bearish (fake pullback).
c) Candle ③: Fully inside Candle ②'s range (**bullish or bearish**).
d) Place a **SELL STOP 1200 points below** the low of **Candle ③**.
e) **Stop Loss: above** the high of Candle ②.

Buy Reversal (After Downtrend):

a) Candle ①: Bearish (momentum).
b) Candle ②: Bullish (fake pullback).
c) Candle ③: Fully inside Candle ②'s range (bullish or bearish).
d) Place a **BUY STOP 1200 points above** the high of Candle ③.
e) **Stop Loss: below** the low of Candle ②.

◆ Weak Signals

- Signal appears during consolidation or inside a range.
- No clear trend exhaustion before the signal.
- Appears too soon after a previous Base Signal (no time for trap setup).

◆ Entry & Stop Loss Strategy

- Use **stop orders only**—never market entries.
- Entry: 1200 points beyond Candle ③'s breakout side (high for buys, low for sells).
- Stop Loss: low/high of the **opposite side** of Candle ②.
- If not triggered within **4-hours**, cancel the order.

◆ Conditions to Confirm the Signal

- There must be a clear prior **trend to reverse**.
- The structure should show **trap behavior**—momentum fading, fake continuation, then pause.
- Price should be reaching a key level (support/resistance, imbalance, supply/demand).
- No large imbalance zones ahead (avoid entering just after **FVGs or** gaps).

◆ Invalid Signals

- The three-candle pattern forms during sideways or choppy price action.

◆ **Order Management**

- Cancel the pending order if it doesn't trigger within 4 hours (or 1 candle on H4).
- If a new signal appears during that time, prioritize the **newest** reversal.

🔍 **Be Observant**

- Look for **trapped momentum**—when the trend slows and suddenly pauses.
- Focus on how Candle ③ behaves: it should show indecision and compression.
- Practice identifying the ①-②-③ trap structure in live charts.

BS7 → Axe

Definition

Base Signal Number Seven, known as **"The Axe,"** is a precision three-candle reversal pattern that forms after an impulsive move and targets trapped liquidity. It begins with a long-wick candle that sweeps key levels, followed by two inside candles—one acting as a fake pullback and the other as a trap confirmation. The Axe is highly effective at key supply/demand or support/resistance zones, where price manipulation is likely.

◆ Signal Logic

The Axe is composed of three distinct candles:

1. **Candle ①:** A long-wicked candle (bullish or bearish body) that sweeps liquidity. The wick shows failed breakout behavior and is essential to the trap setup.
2. **Candle ②:** A smaller candle in the opposite direction (often bullish in a sell setup, bearish in a buy setup), staying within the range of Candle ①. It acts as a **fake pullback** or bait.
3. **Candle ③:** Another small candle, typically in the direction of the trade (e.g., bearish in a sell), still inside the body and wick of Candle ①. It compresses price and finalizes the trap setup.

◆ Signal Criteria

SELL Setup (After Uptrend or Liquidity Grab):

- Candle ①: **Long upper wick** (bullish or bearish body).
- Candle ②: **Bullish**, inside Candle ①'s full range.
- Candle ③: **Bearish** (or neutral), also inside Candle ①'s full range.
- Entry: **SELL STOP** 1200 points below the low of Candle ③.
- Stop Loss: **on the high** of Candle ①.

BUY Setup (After Downtrend or Liquidity Grab):

- Candle ①: **Long lower wick** (bullish or bearish body).
- Candle ②: Bearish, inside Candle ①'s full range.
- **Candle ③**: Bullish (or neutral), also inside Candle ①'s full range.
- Entry: BUY STOP 1200 points above the high of Candle ③.
- Stop Loss: **on the low** of Candle ①.

◆ Weak Signals

• Forms inside consolidation or mid-range price action.
• No strong wick sweep or liquidity grab in Candle ①.
• The three candles are too compressed, showing no clear trap structure.

◆ Entry & Stop Loss Strategy

• Only use **stop orders**—avoid market execution.
• **Entry:** 1200 points beyond the high/low of Candle ③.
• **Stop Loss:** beyond the opposite end of Candle ①.
• Cancel the order if it doesn't trigger within 4hours.

◆ Conditions to Confirm the Signal

• Clear prior **impulse move** or **liquidity sweep** leading into Candle ①.
• Candle ① must have a **long wick** indicating exhaustion.
• Candles ② and ③ **must stay within the full range** of Candle ① (no body breakout).
• Ideally appears at a key level (supply/demand, previous high/low, or imbalance fill).
• No strong imbalance or structural resistance ahead of the entry point.

◆ Invalid Signals

• Candle ② or ③ closes **outside** Candle ①'s range.
• Candle ① wick is not dominant or appears during random price action.
• The structure forms in the middle of a chop zone.

◆ Order Management

• Cancel pending order if not triggered within 4 hours (or 1 candles).
• If a new signal appears within that time, prioritize the **freshest** one.

🔍 Be Observant

• Candle ① is the key—it tells the story of a **trap** through its wick.
• Candle ② gives **false confidence** to counter-trend traders.
• Candle ③ compresses and **sets the trap** before the reversal.
• The Axe is sharp and effective at **key liquidity points**—don't force it in weak zones.
• Practice identifying how all three candles interact with market structure and levels.

BS8 → The Cross

Definition

Base Signal Number Six known as the Cross is a **three-candle reversal pattern** that signals a **momentum shift** at the end of a trend. This setup traps traders expecting continuation, but instead reveals a hidden reversal as the third candle confirms the true direction. It's often seen at exhaustion points where smart money exploits pullback greed before taking the market in the opposite direction.

◆ Signal Logic

This signal traps traders into thinking the pullback (second candle) is a reversal—only for the third candle to confirm the actual reversal in the **opposite direction of the trend**.

It works by:

- Candle ① representing **momentum exhaustion** of the current trend.
- Candle ② appearing to initiate a **pullback**, pulling in early contrarian traders.
- Candle ③ **invalidating** that pullback by **breaking Candle ②'s structure**, confirming a **true reversal**.

◆ Signal Criteria

SELL Signal (Reversal from Uptrend):

- Candle ①: Bearish.
- Candle ②: Bullish (but does not engulf Candle ①).
- Candle ③: Bearish and closes below the low of Candle ②.
- Entry: SELL STOP 1200 points below the low of Candle ③.
- Stop Loss: on opening (or high) of Candle 1.

BUY Signal (Reversal from Downtrend):

- Candle ①: Bullish.
- Candle ②: Bearish (but does not engulf Candle ①).
- Candle ③: Bullish and closes above the high of Candle ②.
- Entry: BUY STOP 1200 points above the high of Candle ③.
- Stop Loss: on the opening of Candle 1.

◆ Weak Signals

- Candle ② engulfs or overpowers Candle ① also makes it invade.
- Candle ③ is small or lacks momentum.
- Pattern appears during **ranging/consolidating** markets.

◆ Entry & Stop Loss Strategy

- Use **stop orders** only (not market orders).
- Entry is placed **1200 points beyond** Candle ③'s breakout wick.
- Stop Loss is set **opening of** Candle 1.
- Candle color on the third candle **must align** with the trade direction.

◆ Conditions to Confirm the Signal

- Must occur **after a clear, mature trend** (not in early trend or sideways market).
- No significant gaps or FVGs invalidating the signal direction.

◆ Invalid Signals

- Candle ② fully engulfs Candle ①.
- Candle ③ fails to break Candle ②'s high/low.
- Appears in tight ranges with low volume or choppy action.

◆ Order Management

- If price doesn't trigger within the next **1 candle on H4**, cancel the order.
- Do not stack multiple signals—only one trade per active signal.

🔍 Be Observant

- Watch how **Candle ② sets the trap**—it shows a false recovery.
- **Candle ③ confirms the reversal**—this is where the real direction is shown.
- Use **FVG zones** to increase confluence and success rate.

BS9 → Range Break

Definition

Base Signal Number Nine, known as **"The T-Wave"** or **"Range Break,"** is a three-candle compression pattern that forms during periods of indecision or equilibrium, often following a trend or corrective wave. The pattern consists of **three candles of nearly identical size** and small or non-existent bodies, signaling the final pause before a **reversal** or **explosive breakout**. The T-Wave represents a hidden battle between buyers and sellers—when resolved, it reveals the true direction and traps those anticipating continuation.

◆ Signal Logic

The T-Wave focuses on price **compression and indecision**.

1. **Three candles** form with **very similar size** and **little to no real body** (mostly wick-based).
2. The candles can alternate in color or be the same; what matters is the **tight size range** and **lack of momentum**.
3. The third candle acts as the **confirmation candle**—a stop order is placed to catch the breakout.
4. Once the breakout occurs, a significant move in the **opposite direction of the prior trend** is expected.

◆ Signal Criteria

BUY Reversal (After Downtrend):

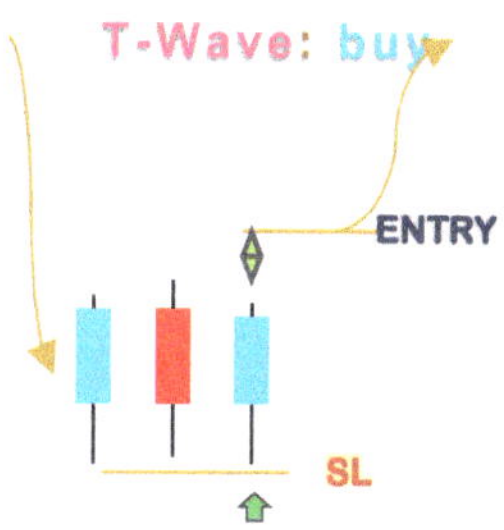

- Candle ①: Bullish or neutral
- Candle ②: Bearish or neutral;
- Candle ③: Bullish or neutral.
- All three candles must have similar size, showing equilibrium.
- Place a BUY STOP 1200 points above the high of Candle ③.
- Stop Loss: below the low of the lowest Candle.

SELL Reversal (After Uptrend):

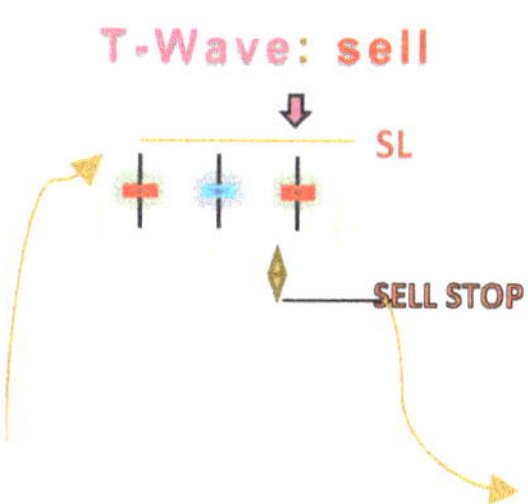

- Candle ①: Bearish or neutral.
- Candle ②: Bullish or neutral.
- Candle ③: Bearish or neutral.
- Same size rule applies tight range, low momentum.
- Place a SELL STOP 1200 points below the low of Candle ③.
- Stop Loss: above the high of the highest Candle.

◆ Weak Signals

• Candles have obvious directional bodies (not neutral enough).
• Uneven candle sizes—breaks the compression logic.
• Signal forms in the middle of a choppy range with no clear prior trend.
• Candle ③ breaks out too early or has imbalance characteristics.

◆ Entry & Stop Loss Strategy

• Always use **stop orders**—never enter at market.
• Entry: 1200 points beyond the breakout side of Candle ③ (high for buys, low for sells).
• Stop Loss: on the dominant Candle.
• Cancel the trade if it doesn't trigger within the next 4hours of the trend continues on its direction breaking out.

◆ Conditions to Confirm the Signal

• Must form after a clear **trend leg** (up or down).
• Three candles must show **size equilibrium**—no dominance.
• Appears at key market structure (supply/demand zone, support/resistance, imbalance zone).
• The breakout should align with a potential trap or exhaustion move.

◆ Invalid Signals

• One or more candles have large directional bodies.
• The three candles vary significantly in length.
• No trend leading into the pattern (flat or sideways).
• Signal contradicts a more dominant or still-active base signal.

◆ Order Management

• Cancel order if not triggered within 4 hours or 1 candle.
• If a newer base signal forms, prioritize that one.
• Avoid re-entries unless another full T-Wave forms with valid structure, renter a reversal.

🔍 Be Observant

• Focus on the symmetry—T-Waves are subtle and easy to overlook.
• Practice spotting candles with nearly **identical length and opposing wicks**.
• Watch how price reacts afterward—**no hesitation** should follow breakout.
• Strongest signals happen when price has just swept liquidity or closed an imbalance.

BS10 → Ghost

Definition

Base Signal Number Ten, known as **"The Ghost"** or **"The Stop Hunt,"** is a deceptive liquidity sweep pattern that occurs at key highs or lows. It involves a long-wicked candle that aggressively hunts stop losses just beyond major levels, followed by a swift rejection. This single-candle setup disguises itself within normal price action, making it difficult to spot without understanding the mechanics of trap-based reversals. "The Ghost" represents smart money manipulation—appearing and disappearing quickly, leaving behind trapped retail orders and a clear direction shift.

◆ Signal Logic

1. **A single candle forms with a long wick** (either above or below), sweeping previous highs/lows or structural zones.
2. The **body of the candle** can be bullish or bearish—it's the **wick** that matters.
3. Think about this as stop hunt, you just opened a trade using one of the base signals either one of the first 9 signal, then you were stop out within 12 hours only to see the market heading back to your direction.

◆ Signal Criteria

SELL Setup (After Stop Hunt High):

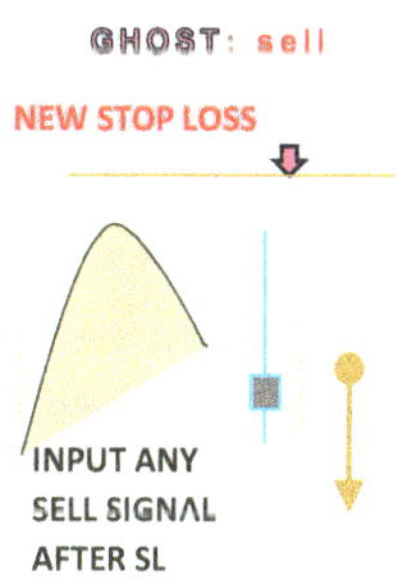

- A single candle forms with a **long upper wick**, hunting your stop loss level of the current sell order predicted by one of the eleven signals.
- Candle body can be bullish or bearish.
- Price should **reject** and close below the previous high.
- Sell immediately after the stop hunt candle closes.
- **Stop Loss**: on the high of the wick.

BUY Setup (After Stop Hunt Low):

- A single candle forms with a **long lower wick**, hunting your stop loss level of the current buy order predicted by one of the eleven signals.
- Candle body can be bearish or bullish.
- Price should **reject** and close back above the previous low.
- Buy immediately after the stop hunt candle closes.
- **Stop Loss**: on the low of the wick.

◆ Weak Signals

- Wick is not significant enough to sweep meaningful liquidity.
- Occurs inside a consolidation or mid-range.
- Candle body dominates the wick (no clear rejection).
- No clear structure or support/resistance near the wick area.

◆ Entry & Stop Loss Strategy

- use market entries.
- Entry: just after the market closes the stop hunt candle
- Stop Loss: beyond the wick's extreme (same side as trap).

◆ Conditions to Confirm the Signal

- Price must hunt your stop loss level of the current order predicted by one of the eleven signals.
- The candle's **wick must be long and aggressive**, signaling a clear stop hunt.
- The body must be positioned **away from the wick direction**, showing rejection.
- Often occurs near previous Base Signals or at major reversal points.

◆ Invalid Signals

• Wick is small or candle closes in the wick's direction.
• No clear high/low taken—just random wick behavior.
• Price consolidates after the signal (no rejection).
• Signal contradicts a still-valid setup from previous base signals.

◆ Order Management

• Prioritize new signals if they appear while the Ghost is pending.
• Ghost signals rarely repeat in the same spot—don't force re-entrics.

🔍 Be Observant

• Ghost candles often appear **fast**—look for impulsive spikes and instant rejections.
• This base signal occurs right after one of the eleven base signal. In other words, it only saves as a re-entry after a stop hunt.
• Watch how volume and speed change during the wick—it should be a sharp move and return.

Phase Five: Test, Manage and Predict

How to Live- and Back-test a Trading Strategy

✅ What is Live Testing?

Live testing (also called forward testing) is the process of applying your trading strategy in real-time market conditions. Live test proves the strategy works in current market and for you. Live testing will help you **understand** the strategy.

✅ What is Back Testing?

Backtesting is a critical step in evaluating and refining a trading strategy. It involves reviewing past market data to see how well your strategy would have performed under actual market conditions. This will help you internalize the strategy and increase your awareness of what to expect during real trading conditions (**knowledge**).

🧠 Why It Matters:

Backtesting tells you if the strategy works in theory.

Live testing tells you if you can actually trade it in real conditions — and whether it's still valid in current market environments.

The steps I've provided break down the process into manageable parts. Below is an outline, with a refined and practical explanation of each step for backtesting and live testing effectively.

Step-by-Step Guide to Back-testing and Live-testing

1. Mark Your Entries and Exits

What to do: Use historical price charts (e.g., June 2–6, 2024) to mark where your strategy would have triggered entries and exits. This can be based on candlestick patterns or other criteria.

How to do it: Use tools like Meta Trader on XMGlobal's platform to scroll back in time. Draw entry and exit lines on the chart. For live testing, set alarms every 4 hours and mark entries/exits in real time.

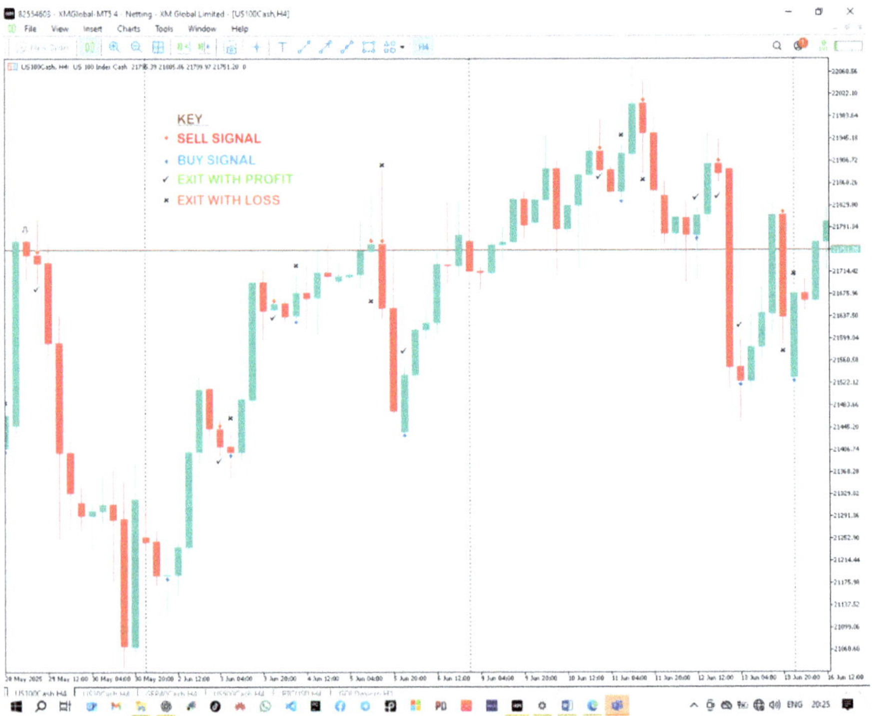

2. Measure the Results

What to do: Calculate the points gained or lost for each trade. Also measure how much drawdown occurred before any profit.

Profit/Loss per Trade: Exit Price – Entry Price (Record as positive for profit, negative for loss).

Down drop (Loss Before Profit): Entry Price – Lowest Price Before Profit. If the trade never became profitable, use total loss. If both loss and drawdown occurred, use the larger of the two.

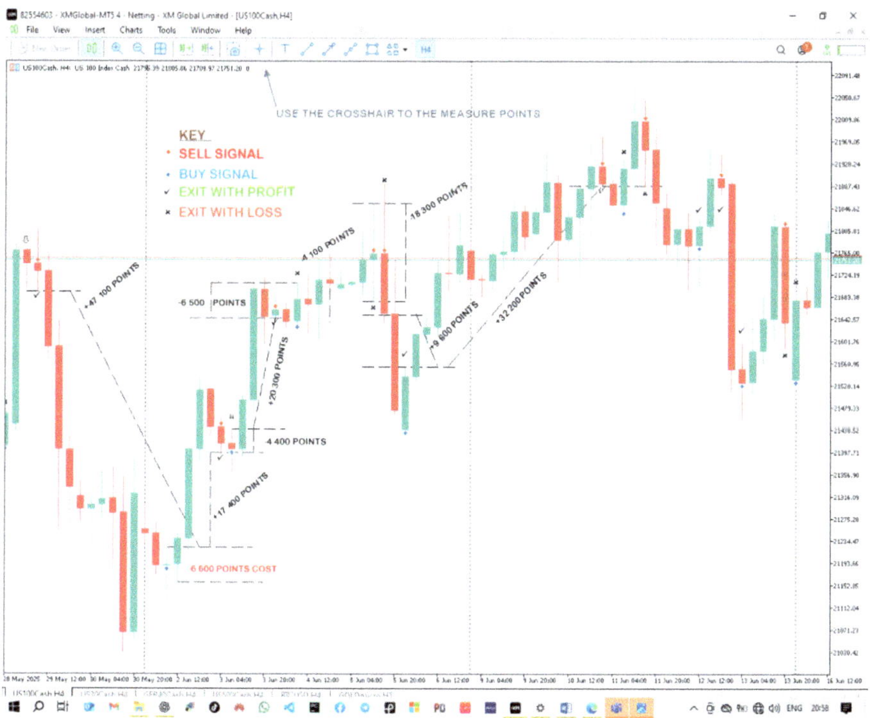

3. Calculate Return and Rejection

Return: Final profit/loss from all trades summed in order.

Rejection: Pullback or worst-case loss during a trade before it moved in your favor.

Down drop: The maximum loss experienced after closing a few orders, typically occurring at the point of lowest return.

$$\text{down drop} = \text{max } \mathbf{rejection} + \text{least } \mathbf{return} \text{ (at max rejection)}$$

Example:

Start at 0 points

Trade 1: +17,400

Trade 2: -4,400 → Total: 13,000

Trade 3: +20,300 → Total: 33,300

Trade 4: -6,500 → Total: 26,800

Trade 5: -4,100 → Total: 22,700

Trade 6: -18,3k→ Total: 4,4k → Rejection = -12k → down drop = -7,6k points

4. Collecting data (All you need from the charts)

◆ Conversion (Points → USD)

Formula: USD = Points × Lot Size × 0.01

Example format {marked in **teal** color}:

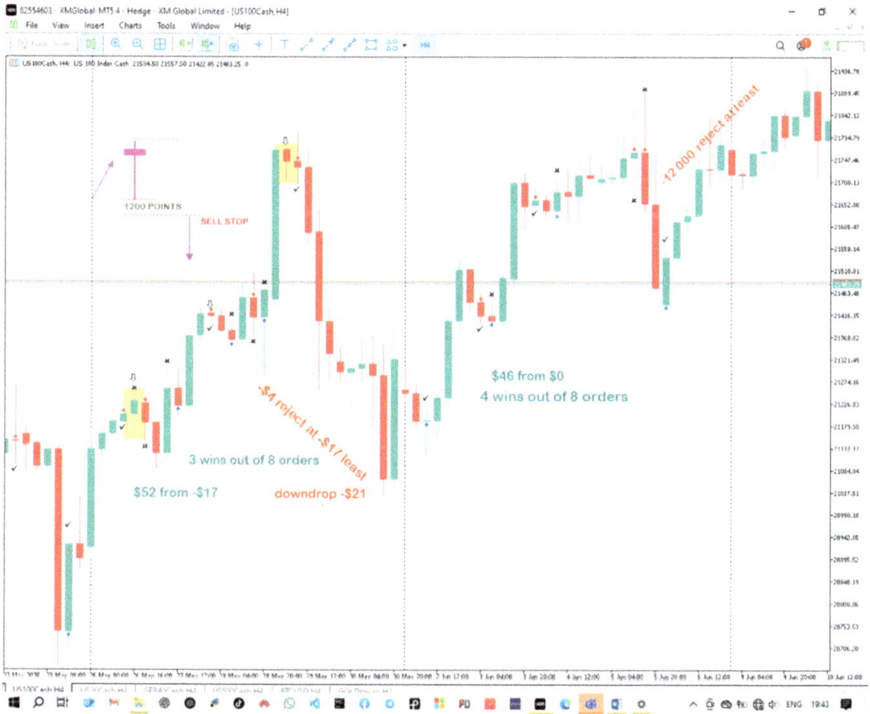

WEEK	ORDERS	WINS	TOTAL RETURN	DOWN DROP
MAY 26–30	8	3	$52	**-$21**
JUNE 02–06	8	4	$46	**-$7.60**
	etc.			

For efficiency, print out the table in this Phase (or draw it in a notebook) and complete it by hand. The following steps will rely heavily on a 0.10 lot size.

🔜 Next Steps

We'll now use the 0.10 lot size to calculate the minimum capital needed to trade US100cash safely — without risking a blown account.

🛡️ 💰 Protection: The Guardian Capital of Account Longevity

Also called:

- **“Sacrificial Margin”**
- **“Protective Capital Buffer”**
- **“Survival Cushion”**
- or in elite trading circles: **“Capital Insurance Layer”**

✨ Definition:

Protection is the **intentional allocation of monetary energy** designed to **absorb the chaos** of real-world market mechanics — slippage, spread erosion, delayed execution, down drops, and volatile spikes — so that your **core capital remains untouched**.

It is not the capital you trade with; it is the capital that **ensures you can keep trading.**

💼 Formulaic Insight:

$$\text{Protection Amount} = \text{Spread} + \text{Down drop}$$

This value should be added to your risk calculation so you **never stake everything on a “perfect setup.”**

📌 Example:

- Spread: 300 points ↦ -$2.40 for 8 orders
- Down drop: -$21
  → **Protection Capital = $23.40**
  That’s what you *pay to survive the game*, not just play it.

Philosophy:

"Protection is not weakness — it is the silent strength that lets your strategy breathe under pressure."

It is the **price of permission to exist** in the market. Without it, even the best strategy will collapse under the weight of noise and randomness.

✍ In Bombastic Terms:

"Protection is the **unsung capital sentinel**, the invisible moat encircling your kingdom of funds. It is the **first cost of war**, the **entry fee into volatility's arena**. Traders who skip this buffer are not bold — they are blind. To protect is not to surrender profit; it is to **defend possibility**."

---

5. Interpreting the data

Someone once said, *"Trading forex doesn't cost a penny."* Sounds nice, right? But let's be real — **that's simply not true**.

Every trade comes with a price. The moment you open a position; you're already paying through the **spread** — the hidden gap between the buy and sell price. And that's not all. **Stop orders**? They may feel like safety nets, but they're not free either. Slippage, early triggers, or market gaps can all eat into your results.

Here's the key: **return is not the same as profit**. Return shows the percentage gain on paper, but **profit is what's left after all the costs are paid** — spreads, slippage, swap fees, everything. That's the number that really counts.

So don't just chase returns. Focus on what you actually get to keep — because **that's the money that grows your account**.

Cost ($) = number of orders × lot × 0.01 × (spread + stop order)
Profit = return + cost

week	spread	down drop	protection	return	cost	profit
30-Dec 2024	$0.90	-$6	= - **$7**	$68	-$5	= $63
Jan 6, 2025	-$1.50	-$41	= - **$43**	-$11	-$8	= - **$19**
Jan 13-17	-$1.50	-$6	= - **$8**	$76	-$8	= $68
Jan 20-24	-$2.10	-$18	= - **$20**	$60	-$11	= $49
Jan 27-31	-$1.50	-$76	= - **$78**	-$75	-$8	= - **$83**
Feb 03-07	-$2.70	-$17	= - **$20**	$17	-$14	= $3
Feb 10-14	-$1.50	-$5	= - **$7**	$38	-$8	= $30
Feb 17-21	-$2.70	-$33	= - **$36**	$10	-$14	= **- $4**
Feb 24-28	-$2.40	-$14	= - **$16**	$65	-$12	= $53
Mar 03-07	-$2.10	-$20	= - **$22**	$38	-$11	= $27
Mar 10-14	-$1.50	-$14	= - **$16**	$108	-$8	= $100
Mar 17-21	-$2.40	-$7	= - **$9**	$55	-$12	= $43
Mar 24-28	-$2.70	-$11	= - **$14**	$72	-$14	= $58
Mar 31 to 4 Apr.	-$2.40	-$115	= - **$117**	$104	-$12	= $92
April 07-11	-$1.80	-$30	= - **$32**	$330	-$9	= $321
April 14-18	-$1.80	-$43	= - **$45**	$57	-$9	= $48
April 21-25	-$1.50	-$7	= - **$9**	$97	-$8	= $89
April 28 to May 2	-$3.90	-$124	= - **$128**	-$69	-$19	= - **$88**
May 05-09	-$2.40	-$75	= - **$77**	-$24	-$12	= - **$36**
May 12-16	-$3.00	-$2	= - **$5**	$76	-$15	= $61
May 19-23	-$1.90	-$7	= - **$9**	$75	-$9	= $66
May 26–30	-$2.40	$21	= - **$23**	$52	-$12	= $40
June 02–06	-$2.40	-$7.60	= - **$10**	$46	-$12	= $34
June 09-13	-$2.10	-$21	= - **$23**	$15	-$11	= $33
Total		-$721				
average		$30.04	**$33.83**		**$10.88**	

6. Holding the line and predicting the future

Deposit = average down drop + average cost + US100Cash minimum equity at 0.10 lot
= 30.04 + 10.88 + 5
= $45.92 = $50
Capital = outlier down drop + maximum cost + deposit
= $124 + $19 + $45.92
= $188,92 = $200

Capital at risk is the protect...just dived into four parts.

Testing the Capital ($200):

		Capital at risk						
Bank	FX Balance	25%	50%	75%	100%	profit	equity	use
150	50	-$7				$ 63	$ 113	63
150	50	-$43				- $ 19	$ 31	
150	31 {-19}	-$8				$ 68	$ 99	49
150	50	-$20				$ 49	$ 99	49
100	50 × 2	-$50	-$38			- $ 83	$ 17	
67	50 {-83}			-$20		$ 3	$ 53	
70	50 {-80}	-$7				$ 30	$ 80	
100	50 {-50}	-$36				- $ 4	$ 46	
100	46 {-54}	-$16				$ 53	$ 99	
149	50 {-1}	-$22				$ 27	$ 77	26
150	50	-$16				$100	$ 150	100
150	50	-$9				$ 43	$ 93	43
150	50	-$14				$ 58	$ 108	58
50	50 × 3	-$50	-$50	-$17		$ 92	$ 242	92
150	50	-$32				$321	$ 371	321
150	50	-$45				$ 48	$ 98	48
150	50	-$9				$ 89	$ 139	89
50	50 × 3	-$50	-$50	-$28		- $ 88	$ 62	
12	50 ×2 {-88}			-$50	-$27	- $ 36	$ 64	
26	50 {-124}	-$5				$ 61	$ 111	
87	50 {-63}	-$9				$ 66	$ 116	3
150	50	-$23				$ 40	$ 90	40
150	50	-$10				$ 34	$ 84	34
150	50	-$23				$ 33	$ 83	33
Total						$1 048	2525	1098
Av.						$ 43.67	105,21	45.75

Predicting the Future

To trade US100Cash based on the first 24 weeks of 2025, you'll need a starting capital of $200. Your deposits will be made in $50 increments, while $150 should be set aside in your bank account as a backup reserve to cover potential outliers.

7. Strategy's performance

📊1. Basic Performance Metrics

✅ Net Profit / Loss

Total loss:
= $19 + $83 $4 + $88 + $36
= $230
Total profit:
= $63+$68+$49+$3+$30+...
= $1 278

- **Formula:**
  Total Profits - Total Losses
  = $1 278 – $230
  = $1 048
- This shows the overall gain or loss.

✅ Return on Investment (ROI)

- **Formula:**
  (Net Profit ÷ Initial Capital) × 100
  = ($1 048÷$200) × 100
  = 524%

- Measures how much return was generated on your capital.

✅ Win Rate

- **Formula:**
  (Number of Winning Trades ÷ Total Trades) × 100
  = (n ÷ 170) ×100
  = x%

- Indicates how often your strategy wins.

✅ Average Win vs. Average Loss

- **Formula:**
  Avg. Win = Total Profit from Wins ÷ Num. of Winning Trades
  = $1278 ÷ n
  = $x per trade
  Avg. Loss = Total Loss from Losses ÷ Num. of Losing Trades
  = $230 ÷ n
  = $x per trade
- Helps understand whether your wins are bigger than your losses.

---

2. *Risk-Adjusted Metrics*

✅ *Sharpe Ratio*

- **Formula:**
  (Avg. Return – Risk-Free Rate) / Standard Deviation of Returns
- Indicates risk-adjusted return; higher is better.

✅ *Sortino Ratio*

- Like Sharpe, but only penalizes **downside volatility**.

✅ *Maximum Drawdown (MDD)*

- **Formula:**
  (Peak Equity - Trough Equity) / Peak Equity
- Shows the largest drop in your account from a peak before a recovery.

✅ *Profit Factor*

- **Formula:**
  Gross Profit ÷ Gross Loss
  = $1 278 ÷ $230
  = 5,5565217391304347
- Values >1 mean your profits exceed losses.

📝 3. Consistency & Efficiency

✅ *Expectancy*

- **Formula:**
  (Win Rate × Avg Win) – (Loss Rate × Avg Loss)
- Measures how much you expect to earn per trade on average.

✅ *R-Multiple / Reward-to-Risk Ratio*

- **Formula:**
  Average Reward / Average Risk
- Shows how much you stand to gain for each dollar risked.

✅ *Trade Frequency & Duration*

- Useful for evaluating whether your strategy is high-frequency or long-term, and how it scales.

8. Planting and Growing your Money Tree

All that profit — even when combined — barely scratches a hundred thousand. And it's frustrating, isn't it? You put in the time, the effort, the discipline… and yet, the numbers still feel small.

So, how do the millionaires do it?

The secret isn't luck. It's not a hidden strategy reserved for the elite. It's something far simpler — **compound interest**.

What truly matters isn't how much you start with, but the **percentage** you can grow consistently. If you can make 10% on a single dollar — just 10 cents — then that same skill can make you 10% on a million, which is $100,000. The math doesn't change. Only the **scale** does.

So, Rozen, are you saying I need a million dollars just to make 100k?

No. That's not what I'm saying at all.

What I'm saying is that you can **build your way there**. You don't need to chase a big lump sum — you need to **compound**. You start with what you have, reinvest your profits, and let those profits start working for you. It's about using your gains to create more gains.

Wealth doesn't come from one big leap. It comes from steady, disciplined growth — from letting time and percentage do the heavy lifting.

Let me show you what that journey could look like, using the previous data.

MONEY GROWS ON TREES:

Money really does grow on trees—if you grow the right one. The same rain that ruins one tree feeds another. Rain is risk. The tree is your system. A strong tree multiplies, casts its own seeds, and bears more fruit. With discipline and print, it turns paper into harvest.

MONEY TREE Standard Edition

📕 Column Logic Explained

Bank

This is your base trading capital at the start of each session. It grows through reinvested profits or resets after a loss or fresh funding. Ideally, keep this capital separate from your active trading account—it acts as insurance against unexpected losses. Think of it as 75% of your total capital, while the trading balance makes up the remaining 25%. For example, if your total capital is $200, your bank would be $150.

Balance

This is the portion of your capital used for active trading—typically 25% of your total capital. The remaining 75% stays in the Bank as protection. If the Bank drops below this 75% threshold, the shortfall is shown in curly brackets {} beside the balance. For example, if your Bank is meant to be $150 but sits at $137, the {13} indicates the deficit.

Risk

This is the maximum amount you're willing to lose in a single trade before profit kicks in. It isn't money set aside—it's the active line between survival and loss. Risk must always be lower than the Balance. If it exceeds the available Balance (after a loss), you draw another 25% from the Bank to restore your trading capacity. This is how the system keeps trading even after the Balance is wiped out—by gradually drawing from the protected Bank reserve.

Lot

Your lot size determines the size of each trade and is calculated by dividing your total capital (Bank + Balance) by 200. This ensures your trade size grows proportionally with your account, balancing growth potential and risk management.

Formula: Lot Size = (Bank + Balance) ÷ 200
i.e. if your total capital is $1,000: Lot Size = 1000 ÷ 200 = 5 lots

Profit

Profit is the earnings from a trade, calculated based on pip movement and lot size or taken directly from trade results. It serves two purposes: to aid recovery after losses, or to fuel growth when no recovery is needed. Tracking profit helps measure your progress and resilience.

Withdraw

The portion of profit you cash out. Helps secure gains outside the trading account. This is used to fuel growth when no recovery is needed.

Save

Save is the total profit retained in your account to support future growth. It only decreases if you move some of it out to add to your trading capital or withdraw it. Otherwise, it remains intact, helping build your trading foundation.

Grow

Grow tracks your account milestones, with each stage (e.g., *2, *4, *8...) representing a new level of growth. Savings—such as $184—are reinvested to fuel continued progress and expand your trading capital. For every $200 in growth, your lot size increases by 0.1, allowing you to scale your trades responsibly.

Bank	Balance	RISK	LOT	PROFIT	WITHDRAW	SAVE	GROW
150	50	7	0.10	63	63	63	
150	50	43	0.10	- 19			
150	31 {-19}	8	0.10	68	49	112	
150	.50	20	0.10	49	49	161	
100	50 × 2	88		- 83			
67	50 {-83}	20		3			
70	50 {-80}	7		30			
100	50 {-50}	36		- 4			
100	46 {-54}	16		53			
149	50 {-1}	22		27	26	187-187	*2
300	87 {-13}	32	0.20	200	187	187-187	*3
450	137 {-13}	27	0.30	129	116	116	
450	150	42	0.30	174	174	290-200	*4
200	200 × 3	468	0.40	368	368	458-400	*6
900	300	32	0.60	1926	1926	1984-ALL	*16
2200	786+200 {-14}	720	1.60	768	754	754-600	*19
2850	950	171	1.90	1691	1691	1845 {45}	*28
1400	1400 × 3	3584	2.80	- 2464		45	
336	1400×2 {-2464}	2156	2.80	- 1008			
728	1400 {-3472}	140	2.80	1708			
2436	1400 {-1764}	252	2.80	1848	84	129	
4200	1400	644	2.80	1120	1120	1249 {49}	*34
5100	1700	340	3.40	1156	1156	1205 {5}	*40
6000	2000	920	4.00	1320	1320	1325{125	*46
6900	2300	1104	4.60	-736		125	
6164	2300 {-736}	1932	4.60	1840	1104	1229{29}	*52
7800	2600		5.20				

📊 Data Interpretation

🔍 Understanding the Columns:

Column	Meaning
Bank	Saved capital or account balance (starting or after reinvestment)
Balance	Typically, the floating or base balance in your fx account
RISK	Required capital allocated per session (in currency)
LOT	Lot size used in the trade
PROFIT	Profit or loss from a trade (negative for losses)
WITHDRAW	Profits withdrawn or cashed out
SAVE	Profits saved or retained
GROW	Overall account growth or milestone achievements (sometimes annotated as * milestones)

📈 General Trend & Interpretation

1. **Consistent Risk Application**:
   - Early stages show strict discipline: Balance mostly locked at 50, LOT at 0.10 — a conservative, beginner strategy.
   - Later, both Balance and lot sizes increase progressively (e.g. 0.10 → 0.20 → ... → 5.20), matching a growth model.
2. **Withdrawal & Save Patterns**:
   - Withdrawals occur mostly after significant profit spikes (e.g. 200, 368, 1926).
   - SAVE column indicates good discipline in retaining profits.
3. **Compounding Strategy**:
   - There are notations like *2, *3, *4 — suggesting a system of milestone multipliers (doubling, tripling accounts etc.).
   - Example:
     - From Bank 149 → 300 → 450 → 900 → 2200 → 2850... a clear path of geometric compounding.
     - These are labeled *2 through *52, indicating stages of growth.

4. **Losses Are Tracked Clearly**:
   - Example: PROFIT of -83, -2464, etc., is integrated and the next rows show adjusted balances.
   - These are used to recalculate SAVE or reset GROWTH logic (e.g. {45} or {29} inside curly braces shows recovery tracking).

🧠 Insights:

- **System-Based Growth**: The *X markers imply a **growth milestone strategy** — where every time a profit goal is met, the risk size, lot size, and bank base grow accordingly.
- **Risk-Reward**: I've applied a **risk ramp-up strategy**, where successful trading leads to higher risk and reward. However, drawdowns (like -2464) show the need for tighter controls as size increases.
- **Capital Reset Points**: When major losses occur (like { -2464}), you switch the bank to a fresh injection or calculation, possibly rebalancing from previous savings.

📌 Sample Interpretation of One Row:

Row with Bank: 900, LOT: 0.60, PROFIT: 1926

- You had $1200 capital, risked $300 (Balance the 25%), used 0.60 lots.
- Trade yielded $1926 profit.
- You withdrew $1926 fully and saved it as part of GROW stage marked 1984-ALL *16.

🔄 *Meaning: Account hit a major growth level (*16), then likely restarted or expanded with saved capital.*

Follow a Scalable, Disciplined Growth Model

*Increase your trade size and risk only as your capital grows. Take profits periodically, mark key growth milestones (using * symbols), and monitor losses carefully. When needed, reset your base and continue with discipline.*

Phase Six: The Test

Assignments:

Assignment 1:

Back test US100Cash, US30Cash, and Ger40Cash (2017 - 2023)

This task is about performing a manual back test for the last **seven years**, from **2017 to 2023**, for three indexes: **US100Cash**, **US30Cash**, and **Ger40Cash**. The goal is to record all the trading results including profits, losses, maximum losses, and average losses or profits.

Assignment 2:

Live Testing

If you've completed this book, you're now ready to proceed with a **16-week live test**.

- **Live Test Setup:**
    - Begin with a demo account or a small real account (e.g., $200 or R3,000 with XM Global). However, the most powerful method is manual practice—tracking trades on paper without risking real money. It sharpens discipline and decision-making like nothing else. Record each order's **performance**, and **weekly results (net points)**.
    - **Objective:** Your goal is to perform **live tests** for **16 weeks** to see how your strategy holds up under real market conditions.

Conclusion:

- **Backtesting**: Critical for testing your strategy's viability over historical data. It helps identify weak spots and areas for improvement.

- **Live Test**: This is the real test. If you can execute the strategy well in live conditions, you prove that you understand risk management, entry/exit strategies, and how to handle real market pressures. Be honest with your testing, and take your results seriously. Remember, **liars lie to themselves** as much as to others. If you're committed to improving, **backtesting** and **live testing** will be your guide.

Phase Seven: Emotions in Forex Trading

Mastering Emotions in Forex

The Problem Isn't Your Emotions — It's What's Triggering Them

Forex is over 83% risk-rated. That means if you trade without strategy, you're gambling—and likely to lose. For a long time, I blamed emotions: stress, depression, frustration. But I later learned that emotions weren't the problem—**my lack of a solid strategy was.**

When you trade without full understanding or confidence, your mind starts creating stories. Doubt creeps in. You fear the loss. You question your setup. That's when emotion takes over—and you make mistakes.

The truth? Emotions don't cause bad trades. Poor planning does.
Emotion is the symptom. Lack of strategy is the disease.

⚠️ The 5 Emotional Traps in Forex

1. Fear of Losing

Fear makes you exit winners too early or hold losers too long. It shows up as:

- Hesitating to enter
- Closing trades too early
- Refusing to accept a loss
- Downsizing out of fear
- Avoiding trades after a loss

Fix it:
Build and test a system you trust. Stick to risk rules. Accept that losses are part of the game, not signs of failure.

---

2. Greed

Greed kicks in after a few wins. You start feeling invincible, break your rules, and chase more.

- Overtrading
- Holding trades too long
- Ignoring your plan
- Overleveraging
- Leaving all profits in the account

Fix it:
Withdraw regularly. Let growth—not emotion—decide your lot size. Celebrate clean execution, not just profit.

---

3. Frustration

After a losing streak, you get emotional. You force trades, break rules, and try to win it back.

- Forcing trades
- Revenge trading
- Changing strategies mid-session
- Blaming the market

Fix it:
Pause. Limit daily trades. Step back and reflect. Focus on the process, not the outcome.

---

4. Hope

Hope keeps you in bad trades, wishing the market will turn.

- Ignoring stop loss
- Holding losers too long
- Trading without a clear plan
- Trusting luck over logic

Fix it:
Hope is not a strategy. Trade only confirmed setups. Plan your trades and accept losses with discipline.

---

5. Ego

Ego makes you need to be right—even if it breaks your system.

- Refusing to close losing trades
- Getting overconfident after wins
- Thinking you're smarter than the market
- Trading to prove a point

Fix it:
The market rewards humility, not pride. Let the system win, not your ego. Learn from every mistake.

🛠 How to Trade Without Emotion

1. Build a Real Plan
Define your entries, exits, risk, and rules. Stick to them.

2. Accept Losses
Losses are the cost of trading. Manage them wisely—don't fear them.

3. Control Your Mindset
Step away when emotions rise. Reset before trading again.

4. Focus on the Long Game
This is a marathon, not a sprint. Stay consistent over time.

5. Keep Evolving
Journal, review, and refine. Never stop learning.

6. Trust Your System
If you've tested it—use it. Don't trade on impulse.

🎯 Final Words: Beat Yourself, Not the Market

The real opponent in forex isn't the market—it's you. Master yourself, and the market will eventually reward you.

Money isn't emotional. It responds to structure, discipline, and strategy.
Trade the setup. Trust the process. Leave emotion at the door.

Phase Eight: Psychology

Subconscious LAWS – Frank Oatlew Said:

Law of Awareness:

- **Observe your thoughts**, because they will become your actions.
- **Observe your actions**, because they will become your habits.
- **Observe your habits**, because they will become your nature.
- **Observe your nature**, because it will determine your destiny.

You will **never reach your full potential** until you learn to **act in sync with what you believe**. Whatever strategy you choose, make sure you **believe in it completely**. Only then can you fully commit to it and avoid **self-sabotage**. You will act in alignment with what you truly believe in by utilizing the law of **repetition**. Repetition is the key to mastering both your strategy and your mindset. If you can't see yourself succeeding with your current plan, then it's time to rethink your strategy. When you believe in something, you act on it confidently.

Law of Attraction:

- **Birds of a feather flock together!**

- People naturally attract each other based on shared interests, energy, and lifestyle. This law governs the subconscious mind—making us gravitate toward people, ideas, and energies that reflect what we carry inside us.

If you are a **positive person**, you'll find that positive people will surround you. **Positivity breeds more positivity**—that's the law at work. **So, if you find yourself surrounded by negativity**, distance yourself from it for a while. It's not about abandoning people, but **about finding your own clarity**. Think of it as stepping off a sinking ship to fix your own boat, so when you return, you can help everyone. **This applies not just to people, but to your systems and strategies**. If you've been using a strategy that hasn't worked, **don't just stick with it** because of faith. **Keep it simple** until you start seeing consistent results.

Law of Reflection:

- **Kindness and sincere courtesy** are the best gifts you can offer to anyone. And even if someone can't immediately repay your kindness, rest assured it will return to you, perhaps at another time.

- **Internally**, the subconscious appreciates kindness, and it will reflect back in your life, often in surprising ways. **The law of reflection** works through our relationships—when someone gives you a gift, you feel compelled to return it, often with something of equal or greater value. This is how the universe operates. **The energy you put out will come back to you**—so make sure it's the right energy!

- Winning isn't a coincidence—it's a **choice**! If you don't believe that, then by default, you believe you have no control over your destiny. **If that's true, then what's the point of even trying? But let me tell you, you do have control**, and that control lies in your actions and your beliefs. So, **be kind and gentle in your approach**. Don't chase after the market or overtrade. **Forex trading is not the problem—your approach is the solution.**

Law of Focus:

- **What you focus on, you will get!**

- When you focus on **negative things**, you'll attract more negativity. Just like when you sit with a friend who is always unhappy—they only see the world through a lens of misery, even in casual conversations. You'll find they're speaking about how bad their day is, and in the end, everything seems like a disaster.

- **Your focus shapes your reality**. If you focus on **growth, learning, and opportunity**, you will start seeing more of those things in your life and in your trading. The truth is, **everyone has a champion trader inside of them**. It's just a matter of **knowledge**, **desire**, and **commitment**. **Now, focus on the future**. Focus on the opportunities ahead, not on past mistakes. **Be positive about your losses** and learn from them, because they'll make your future wins that much sweeter.

Law of Expectation:

- Similar to the **Law of Focus, expectations are powerful**. This law governs the way our subconscious anticipates outcomes based on what we believe.

- For example, if you go into an exam expecting failure, you'll find reasons to fail—your mindset will shape your actions. The same goes for trading: **if you expect to lose, you'll subconsciously make decisions that bring about that loss**.

- **Your expectations directly impact your results**. I can tell you about my experience back in 2019 when I was doing matric. I dropped out after Term 3, but still managed over 70% on my math prelims and improved to 50% higher on my final exam—**without a calculator**! It wasn't because I was lucky; it was because I had trained my subconscious to expect success.

- In trading, you can build your expectations through **repetition and practice**. Doing the tests will help you **know what to expect** when you trade, so you're not relying on hope or chance. It's about creating **predictability** and confidence in your strategy.

Law of Belief:

- **You focus, you expect, and then it happens**. Repeatedly.

- Success is not a **random occurrence**. It's a **purposeful pursuit**. If you want to become rich, you must believe that you will. **You will not get rich by accident**. You will get rich **by design**, by following a clear path and purpose.

- This is why I've told you **to live test my strategy for at least seven weeks**. If you **don't believe in it**, then don't waste your time. You have to **believe in your approach** and **trust it to work**. Your belief will shape your actions, and in turn, your success.

Law of Accumulation and Habits:

- The subconscious mind works on the principle of **accumulation**. **What you repeat, you will believe**. Anything that becomes a habit was **accumulated through repetition**. Over time, your thoughts, words, and actions shape your subconscious mind.

- **Repetition** is key. **The more you repeat something, the more it becomes automatic**. This is why you need to **repeat your strategy over and over** until it becomes second nature.

- **This is also why I recommend using the alarms** I've given you for the first two weeks. As you practice, you'll start waking up even before your alarms—this is the power of repetition and habit. **Your mind will naturally adapt** and the strategy will become part of you.

- You will be **shocked** when you realize how simple it can be to accumulate wealth, but **don't take risks** and invest blindly. **Do not overestimate the strategy's effectiveness**—it has its downsides too. **Don't overtrade**. This is why you must pass the test before diving into real trading. You **must accumulate your knowledge and make this a habit** before you risk your capital.

Law of Replacement:

- To change the beliefs in your subconscious, **you have to replace them**, because there's no way to simply **delete** old beliefs. You can only **replace** them with new, empowering beliefs.
- **Replace destructive habits with positive ones**. Replace the belief that you can't succeed with the belief that you **are capable of succeeding. You are your habits**—so shape them.
- This applies to your trading mindset too: **if you don't know how to control your emotions, how will you control your trades?** Most traders lose money because they cannot control their emotions and their impatience. They make impulsive decisions, and that's where the real danger lies.
- **Don't exit your trades randomly**. Only exit when the conditions are right—when your strategy tells you to. Don't close trades just because you "feel" like it. **Trust your system**.
- Your trades should reflect your discipline, not your emotional impulses. **Become a professional**. Don't hedge or trade recklessly. Organize yourself, set alarms, and **stick to the plan**.
- **I expect you to approach trading like a professional**. A trader with a clear strategy, **not a gambler**. This is not about mixing strategies. This is about **dedicating yourself to one approach**, and mastering it.

Conclusion:

If you want to control your destiny, you must first control your mind. **Subconscious laws** govern everything, from your thoughts to your actions. **Master these laws, and you will become a master of your life and your trades**.

Phase Ten: Bonus

You Don't Need Full Capital to Get Started Anymore!

The good news is; you **don't need the full capital** to begin your trading journey anymore. XMGlobal is offering a **100% deposit bonus**. This means instead of needing the entire **$200** upfront, you can start with just **$100**.

Here's how it works:

1. **Register your account with XMGlobal**.
2. **Submit your documents** for verification.
3. Once approved, make a **deposit of $100**.
4. Your deposit will be **doubled with a 100% bonus**, giving you the **minimum equity required** to start trading with the strategy I've shared.

This **bonus** is a great way to get started without having to risk your full capital right away. It lowers the entry barrier, allowing you to **trade smartly** and **learn at your own pace**.

Bonus: Additional Signals for Your Benefit

I've also included **some additional signals** for you, which will enhance your trading experience. These will help you make more informed decisions and ensure that you're on the right track.

Remember, the goal is to stay consistent and stick to the strategy. **This is just the beginning**, and with time, patience, and the right mindset, you'll begin to see the results you're working for.

Good luck, and keep going! You're on your way to mastering your trading strategy.

BS1 → Impulse Catcher

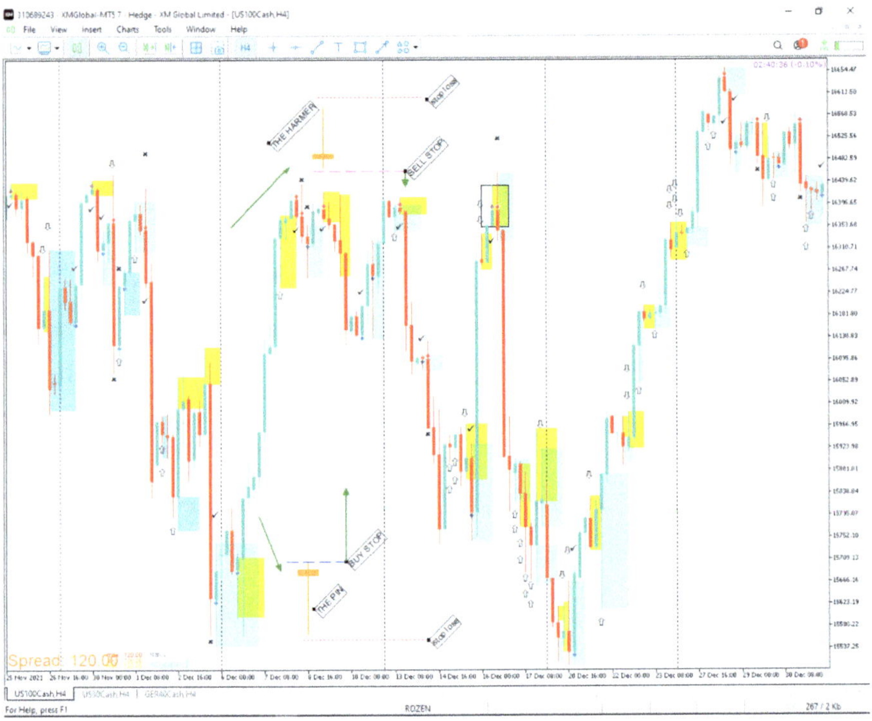

Definition:

Base Signal Number One is a single-candle trading signal primarily derived from *hammer candlesticks*. This signal is used to identify potential reversals and is most effective when confirmed by structure and market behavior.

◈ *Signal Criteria*

SELL Signal (Bearish Reversal)

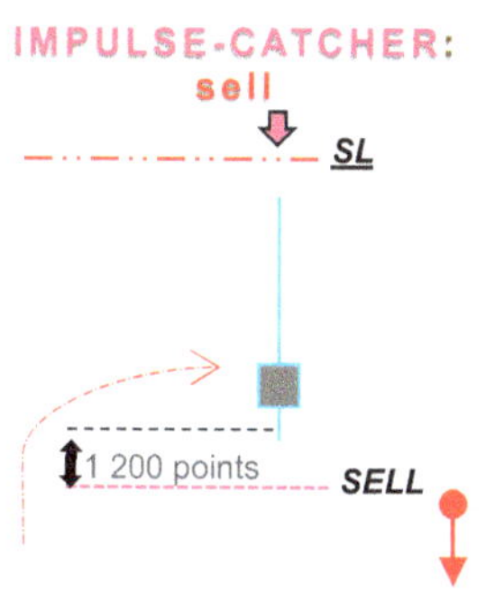

- The upper wick must be longer than both the body and the lower wick.
- The longer upper wick reflects strong bearish rejection.
- The candle should ideally appear higher than previous candles for added strength.

BUY Signal (Bullish Reversal)

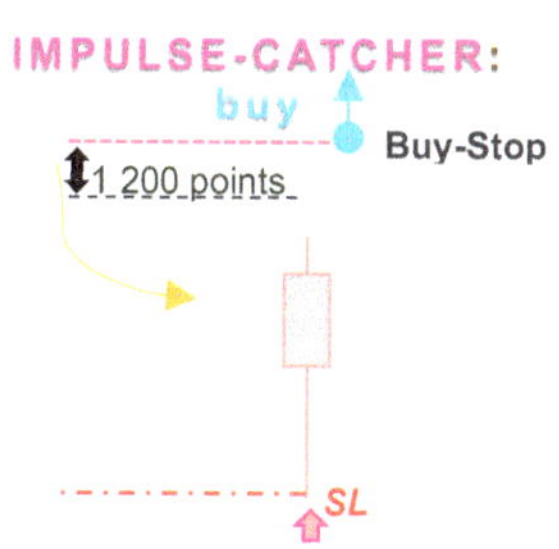

- The lower wick must be longer than both the body and the upper wick.
- The longer lower wick indicates strong bullish rejection.
- The candle should ideally appear lower than previous candles for added strength.

◈ *Weak Signals*

- **Inside candlesticks** (small bodies within previous candle ranges) are considered **weak**.
- A weak **sell** signal: candle is lower than previous but not clearly dominant.
- A weak **buy** signal: candle is slightly higher but lacks momentum.

◈ *Entry & Stop Loss Guidelines*

- **Use stop orders** (not market execution) to avoid traps and fake-outs.
- **Place your stop order 1,200 points** away from the **shorter wick**.
- **Place your stop loss** on the **high of the candle** for a **sell signal** and on the **low** for a **buy signal of the candle**.
- If a **stop hunt** occurs and you're taken out, **re-enter immediately** on confirmation. **Wait for the stop hunt candle to close first.**
- The type of candle (bullish, bearish, or doji) doesn't matter—as long as one wick is significantly longer than both the body and the other wick.

◈ *Market Conditions to Avoid*

- **To trade** during **abnormally large, tiny candles, ranging, consolidation or large unfilled gaps** (Fair Value Gaps or FVG) study **trading the rough zone**.
- Ensure that the **previous signal is still in profit** before entering a new one for **strong signal**.
- Only take **reversal trades**, not continuation setups unless a **stop hunt** occurred.

◈ *Invalid Signals*

- A signal that **doesn't oppose** the previous dominant move is considered **invalid**.
- Always analyze the **previous signal that moved the market** to avoid taking **invalid signals**.

◈ *Trade Management Rules*

- If the stop order is **not triggered within 4 hours**, **manually delete** the order.
- If another opposite Base Signal One appears **within 12 hours' even if the previous signal had not moved** to the **desired direction** after being triggered, place a **new stop order** in the opposite direction—this usually reflects a **pullback or retest**.

◈ *Order Management*

- If the **next few candles** fail to break the signal candle's range, you may reclassify it as a valid **Base Signal** respectively (see Base Signal Number Seven).
- If price action supports the signal but doesn't trigger your order, consider **adjusting the stop order for a better entry** respectfully (see **Base Signal Number Six**).

🔍 Observation & Confirmation

- Carefully observe wick structure and candle positioning.
- Be sure the signal aligns with market momentum and structural reversal areas.
- Wait for confirmation and avoid impulsive entries.

Coming up next: Inverse

BS2 → Wick Trap

Definition:

Base Signal Number Two is called the Wick Trap is a single-candle reversal signal, conceptually derived from the **hammer** candlestick formations. It acts as a reversal of **Base Signal Number One** and focuses on **market manipulation traps** and **momentum shifts**.

◈ *Signal Logic*

If a candle forms with a **long lower wick**, it typically indicates **strong bullish rejection**, suggesting upward momentum. However, if the market **continues to push downward afterward**, this contradicts that bullish signal—and that's your opportunity to **sell**.

◈ *Signal Criteria*

SELL Signal (Hanging Man)

- The **lower wick** must be **longer** than the upper wick and the candle body.
- This implies **fake bullish pressure** followed by a downward reversal.
- The candle should appear **higher** than previous candles to indicate a potential **top**.

BUY Signal (Inverted Hanging Man)

- The **upper wick** must be **longer** than both the lower wick and the body.
- This indicates **fake bearish pressure** before a reversal upward.
- The candle should be **lower** than previous candles to signal a potential **bottom**.

◈ Weak Signals

A signal is weak when the candle is an **inside bar**—not exceeding the range of the previous candle.

- For a **sell**: the candle is lower or smaller, offering weak confirmation.
- For a **buy**: the candle is slightly higher or lacks wick dominance.

◈ Entry & Stop Loss Strategy

- Always **use stop orders** (not market entries) to reduce the chance of being caught in fake moves.
- **Stop orders** should be placed **on the high or low longer wick respectively**.
- **Place your stop loss** on the **high of the candle** for a **sell signal** and on the **low** for a **buy signal of the candle**.
- If you experience a **stop hunt, re-enter immediately** once price action confirms reversal. **Wait for the stop hunt candle to close first.**
- The candle can be **bullish, bearish, or a doji**—what matters is that **one wick is clearly longer than both the body and the opposite wick**.

◈ *Conditions to Confirm the Signal*

- The market must not be **ranging** or **consolidating**.
- There should be **no major gaps (Fair Value Gaps / FVG)** before the candlestick.
- The **previous signal should still be in profit**—only trade one active signal at a time.
- **Only trade reversal signals, not continuation** patterns.
- Avoid **abnormally large or tiny candles** as they carry higher risk—refer to the **rough zone** section for clarity.

◈ *Invalid Signals*

- A signal that **doesn't contradict** the last dominant move is invalid.
- Always analyze the **previous Base Signal** before entering to ensure alignment with trend exhaustion and reversal potential.

◈ *Order Management*

- If the order **has not triggered within 4 hours**, delete it manually.
- If price action supports the signal but doesn't trigger your order (see **Base Signal Number Six**).

🔍 Be Observant

- Focus on wick size, body size, and candle position relative to recent structure.
- Be patient and wait for confluence between wick logic and price movement.
- Mastery of this signal requires **live observation** and reference to the **evidence images**.

BS3 → Twins

Definition

Base Signal Number Three also known the power called the twins is a two-candle reversal formation that emphasizes momentum exhaustion after aggressive price moves. It is designed to catch smart money traps where a strong impulsive candle is immediately followed by an equal or stronger opposing candle—indicating a potential market reversal. This signal is built on the concept of liquidity grabs and false breakouts.

◈ *Signal Logic*

Base Signal Number Three highlights a market trap where traders are lured into a false breakout, only for the market to reverse sharply. The first candle shows strong directional momentum (bullish or bearish), while the second candle rejects that move entirely. This rapid contradiction signals that institutional traders may have filled positions and reversed the flow.

◈ *Signal Criteria*

SELL Signal (Bearish Reversal Block):

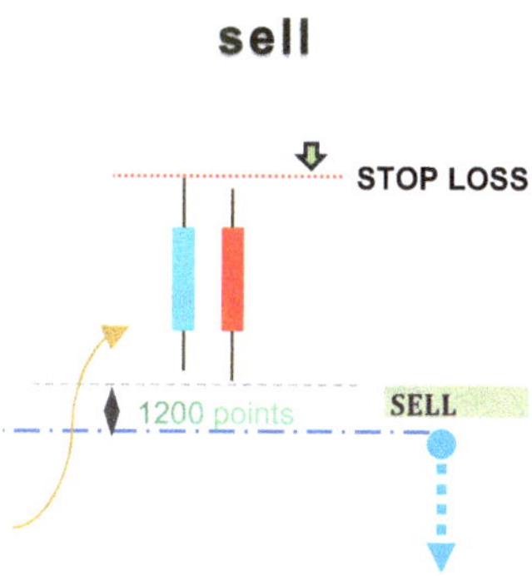

- **The first candle must be a strong bullish candle (large body, small wicks).**
- **The second candle must open at the close of the first and close below its open (engulfing).**
- **Ideally, the second candle should have a body that covers at least *101*% of the first candle's body.**
- **The signal should appear near after an extended bullish run.**

BUY Signal (Bullish Reversal Block):

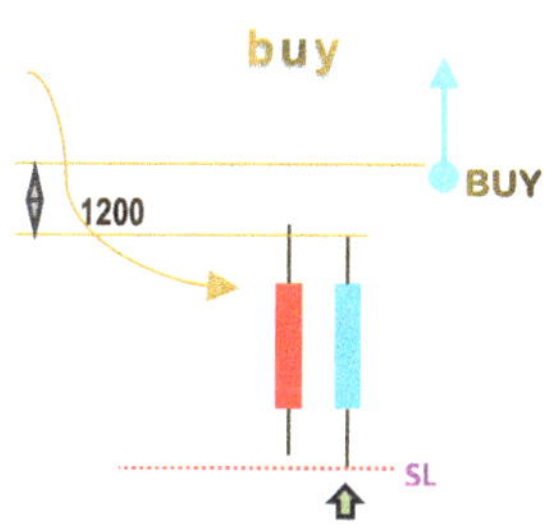

- The first candle must be a **strong bearish candle** (large body, small wicks).
- The second candle must open below or at the close of the first and close above its open (**engulfing**).
- Ideally, the second candle should have a body that covers at least *101*% of the first candle's body.
- The pattern should appear near a recent low or after a sharp decline.

◈ *Weak Signals*

- The second candle fails to engulf at least 100% of the first candle's body.
- The formation appears in a tight range or consolidation zone.
- There is no clear trend exhaustion or structural confluence (e.g., not near a support/resistance zone).
- The two candles are too small to suggest meaningful market participation.

◈ *Entry & Stop Loss Strategy*

- Place a **stop order** just beyond the wick of either the first or second candle (1200 points distance recommended).
- Stop Loss should be placed beyond the opposite wick of the formation.
- Avoid market entries—wait for breakout confirmation.
- If the price breaks opposite side of the formation and then returns inside, delete the order manually.
- Re-enter only when the structure had a stop hunt base signal.

◈ *Conditions to Confirm the Signal*

- The two candles must represent a clear momentum reversal.
- The price should be reacting off a key structure (support/resistance, supply/demand zone).
- Avoid entering during consolidation or in the middle of a trading range.
- There should be no unfilled Fair Value Gaps (FVG) immediately before the signal.

◈ *Invalid Signals*

- The second candle fails to close beyond 99.9% of the first candle.
- The signal appears mid-range with no clear trend leading up to it.
- It contradicts the overall structure or ignores recent key levels.

◈ *Order Management*

- If a new Base Signal appears within **12 hours**, follow that instead.
- If price consolidates around the entry zone without triggering, consider revalidating with nearby signals like Base Signal Six.
- If signal is still valid but un-triggered, you may delete in four hours.

🔍 *Be Observant*

- Focus on the **contrast between the two candles**—momentum shift must be obvious.
- Check for liquidity zones that may have been swept before the reversal.
- Watch out for strong rejection wicks on the second candle to confirm reversal intent.
- Patience is critical—don't anticipate the signal, wait for clear confirmation.

Phase Ten: Trading the Rough Zones

Overcoming Disturbances and Disruptions in Your Trading

The Market and Profitability

If you've been paying attention to the tests you've done—or the ones, you'll do—you'll notice a pattern: **The market only rewards you with profits when it's not ranging or when liquidity is normal.** When candles are ranging, the market is full of noise, and that noise leads to **too many mixed signals**. This makes it harder to predict the market and trade effectively.

I've identified a solution to **lower the noise**, and in doing so, I've realized that **market noise isn't the only disturbance you face**. There are other personal and subconscious disruptions that can affect your trading.

Common Disturbances and Solutions

Sexual Violation and Imposed Beliefs

Sexual violation and imposed beliefs may not seem relevant to trading, but let me explain. Sometimes, when a trade seems too easy, it could be a **signal for underlying emotional distractions**, like sexual violation. Let me be clear—trading should not be hard, but **sexual violation** is an invisible factor that can affect your mental and emotional state.

Sexual violation refers to any form of **sexual misconduct** that crosses boundaries, and it doesn't only affect children; it affects everyone. These actions can disrupt your mindset and lead to poor decisions. I want to emphasize that **sex drive** can be a loophole for many, and if you're not careful, it may distract you from focusing on your trading decisions.

In the world we live in, we're bombarded by various manipulations. A simple example of this is how the **stock market** is structured. The market was never designed to make the average person wealthy; it was structured to keep the poor poorer and the rich richer. But how do the **10% who succeed** manage to make it?

It's all about **manipulation**. Advertisers and media create "hidden messages" that target your subconscious mind. These messages are designed to shape your beliefs and desires without your conscious awareness. So, ask yourself—why do you buy into these manipulations?

Here's the truth:

1. **Money isn't evil**—but the way it's portrayed in the media can make you think it is. The more you believe that the rich get their wealth through dishonest means, the more you'll sabotage your own chances of success.
2. **Drug abuse**—Hollywood glamorizes substance abuse. The truth is, success doesn't come from drugs, but from hard work and balance.
3. **Sexual weakness**—you were never meant to be driven by your sexual desires. **Stay alert** and focus on what's real. Love should be **balanced**, not obsessive. Your success doesn't hinge on the approval or fantasies of others.

Emotional Heartbreak and Self-Sabotage

Another factor is **emotional heartbreak**. We all experience feelings, and sometimes we act on them, but when you're feeling emotional, it's critical to **stay away from trading**. Emotional distress clouds judgment. If you're feeling sad, angry, or hurt, you're not in the right mental state for making rational decisions.

Here are some signs of emotional heartbreak:

- **Pretending to be fine when you're not**
- **Judging others**
- **Overdoing tasks or house chores**
- **Moody behavior**
- **Lack of appetite or constant wishful thinking**

Solution: **Focus on yourself.** Don't compare yourself to others. Do not get stuck on perfection, because none of us are perfect. Go for a walk or **hit the gym**. Physical activity can clear your mind.

Spiritual Infections and Their Impact on Trading

You may go to church on Sunday, feeling spiritually connected, and by Monday, you're making irrational decisions in the market. You may even **pray** that your account won't blow up, but those prayers won't fix bad decisions. It's not about your beliefs; it's about your actions.

Spiritual infections can come in the form of **over-reliance on faith** without practical action. This can cause **self-sabotage**, and you'll find yourself **praying for the market** instead of taking logical steps to manage risk.

Signs of spiritual infections include:

- Praying for the market to turn in your favor
- **Talking without taking action**
- **Self-sabotage** and lack of practical strategy
- Being too **one-sided** in your approach to life and trading
- **Neglecting logic** in favor of blind faith

Solution:

Balance is key. You need to balance your spiritual life with your emotional, mental, and physical well-being. Know the **differences** between your spiritual beliefs and practical decisions.

Final Thoughts

At the end of the day, all of these disturbances can **hold you back** from reaching your full potential in trading and in life. They can distract you from focusing on **what really matters**—the right strategy, the right mindset, and maintaining emotional balance.

The **real solution** is to **stay grounded**. Avoid getting lost in the noise, whether it's market fluctuations, personal distractions, or societal pressures. Stay focused, stay disciplined, and **build your wealth in alignment with your values**.

The only person who can truly change your life is **you**. Don't let external influences, emotions, or manipulations control your decisions. Recognize the signs of **disturbance** and take action. You're in control, and you have the power to change your outcome.

Major Signals vs. Minor Signals

Mixed signals are an inevitable part of trading. No matter how much experience you gain, you will face times when signals seem contradictory. However, these signals are not just random; they can be categorized into **major** and **minor** signals.

- **Major signals** are more significant and reliable, while **minor signals** are smaller, less decisive, and often appear **inside** the major signals.
- When faced with a mixed signal situation, a good practice is to **use stop orders** to help you manage risk. This helps you avoid entering a position prematurely or chasing signals that are not clear.

The images I've included will help you visualize these concepts more effectively. Pay attention to how the minor signals always seem to fit within or around the major signals—they might even seem like "false signals," but they offer useful information when used correctly.

If you see two candles showing opposite momentum, you're dealing with mixed signals. Avoid trading within this zone, as the market lacks clear direction. Instead, highlight long wicks and wait for breakouts before entering a trade.

Do not reenter trades just because a signal continues—always wait for a proper exit before considering an opposite trade.

Sometimes, you'll get two conflicting signals. In such cases, the major signal usually carries stronger momentum. Even within mixed signals, you might identify a major and minor signal. While it's possible to trade within mixed zones or on wicks, these setups are riskier than waiting for a clean breakout.

310689243 - XMGlobal-MT5 7 - Netting - XM Global Limited - [US100Cash,H4]
File View Insert Charts Tools Window Help
H4
mixed signal
major signals
minor signal(s)
invalid signals
profit loss
Line Studies
down trend
Spread: 120.00
US100Cash,H4
US30Cash,H4
GER40Cash,H4
US100Cash,H1
For Help, press F1
ROZEN
0 / 0 Kb

310689243 - XMGlobal-MT5 7 - Netting - XM Global Limited - [US30Cash,H4]
File View Insert Charts Tools Window Help
COVERING THE GAPES
BUY INDICATION SELL
BUY INVALID SELL
BUY WEAK SELL
MIXED SINAL
BULLISH ENGULFING
Line Studies
MIXED SIGNALS
Spread: 120.00
US100Cash,H4 US30Cash,H4 GER40Cash,H4 US100Cash,H1
For Help, press F1

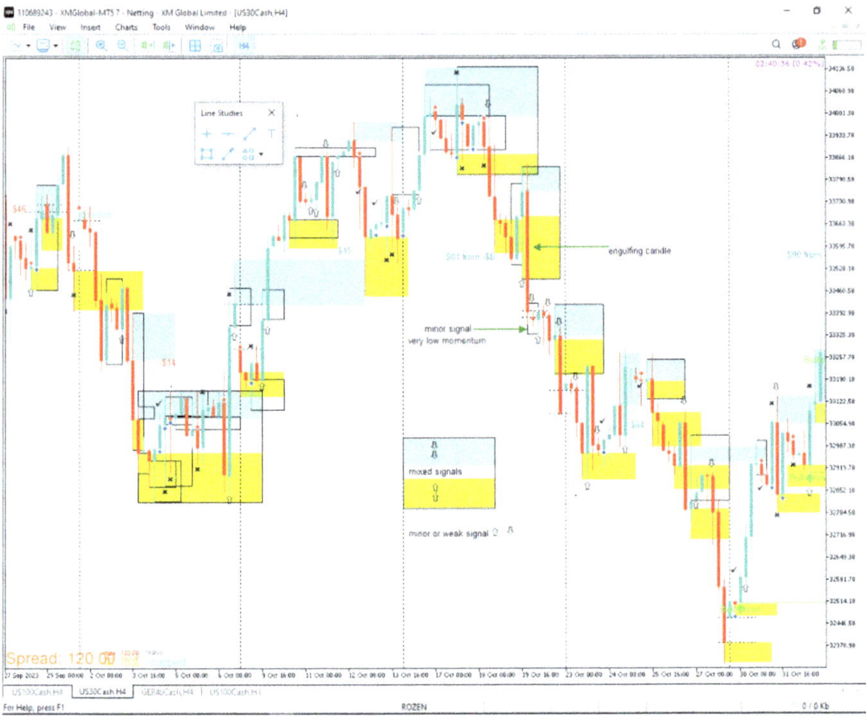
File
View
Insert
Charts
Tools
Window
Help
Line Studies
engulfing candle
minor signal
very low momentum
mixed signals
minor or weak signal
Spread: 120.00
US30Cash,H4
For Help, press F1

Long Wicks and the Stop Hunt

When big news events or market shifts occur, you may see **long wicks** in the candlesticks. These can sometimes be misleading, hitting your **stop loss** or changing the market's direction unexpectedly.

This can throw off your trade and cause you to:

- Lose direction of the market.
- Close profits prematurely (before they turn into larger profits).

In our strategy, a **stop hunt** is a common phenomenon. A stop hunt happens when the market moves quickly to hit a significant number of stop-loss orders before reversing direction. You can spot this as the continuation of the strategy we discussed earlier, especially if you had your stop loss set correctly.

An example of this is when you see a **long wick with a small body** on the candlestick chart—like the **axe** pattern I mentioned in the previous strategy phase. Make sure to look closely at the upcoming pictures to get a better understanding.

A **long upper wick** indicates strong **bearish momentum**, while a **long lower wick** signals strong **bullish momentum**—regardless of whether the candle itself is bullish or bearish. The most significant candles typically have a **small body** compared to the longest wick, assuming the candle has wicks on both ends. In contrast, a candle with **equal-length wicks** gives **mixed signals** and lacks clear directional strength.

310689243 - XMGlobal-MT5 7 - Netting - XM Global Limited - [GER40Cash,H4]
File View Insert Charts Tools Window Help
H4
STRONG BEARISH MOMENTUM
UPPER WICK
OR
BEARISH
INDICATION GAPE
Line Studies
BULLISH
INDICATION GAPE
OR
LOWER WICK
STRONG BULLISH MOMENTUM
Spread: 120.00
13562.37
13534.54
13506.71
13478.88
13451.05
13423.22
13395.39
13367.56
13339.73
13311.90
13284.07
13256.24
13228.41
13200.58
13172.75
13144.92
13117.09
13089.26
13061.43
13033.60
13005.77
12977.94
12950.11
12922.28
12894.45
12866.62
12838.79
12810.96
12783.13
12755.30
12727.47
12699.64
12671.81
12643.98
12616.15
22 Aug 2022
23 Aug 20:00
25 Aug 04:00
26 Aug 12:00
29 Aug 20:00
31 Aug 04:00
1 Sep 12:00
2 Sep 20:00
6 Sep 04:00
7 Sep 12:00
8 Sep 20:00
12 Sep 04:00
13 Sep 12:00
14 Sep 20:00
16 Sep 04:00
US100Cash,H4
US30Cash,H4
GER40Cash,H4
US100Cash,H1
For Help, press F1
ROZEN
0 / 0 Kb

The Trend – Patience is Key

As we've discussed before, just because you receive a signal to **buy** or **sell**, it doesn't mean you should immediately act on it. The market moves in **phases**, and not every signal is confirmed.

Key Point:

- **Don't act on a signal until it's confirmed.**
- If you notice a signal forming, but it hasn't confirmed yet, **wait** before taking any action. Patience is your ally. Once confirmation comes in, then you can act decisively, like a lion waiting for the right moment to strike.

The tendency to think the market will always go **up** and then **come down** is a common mistake. In reality, the market might just keep going up without ever retracing. **We follow the market**—we are **not market makers**, but traders.

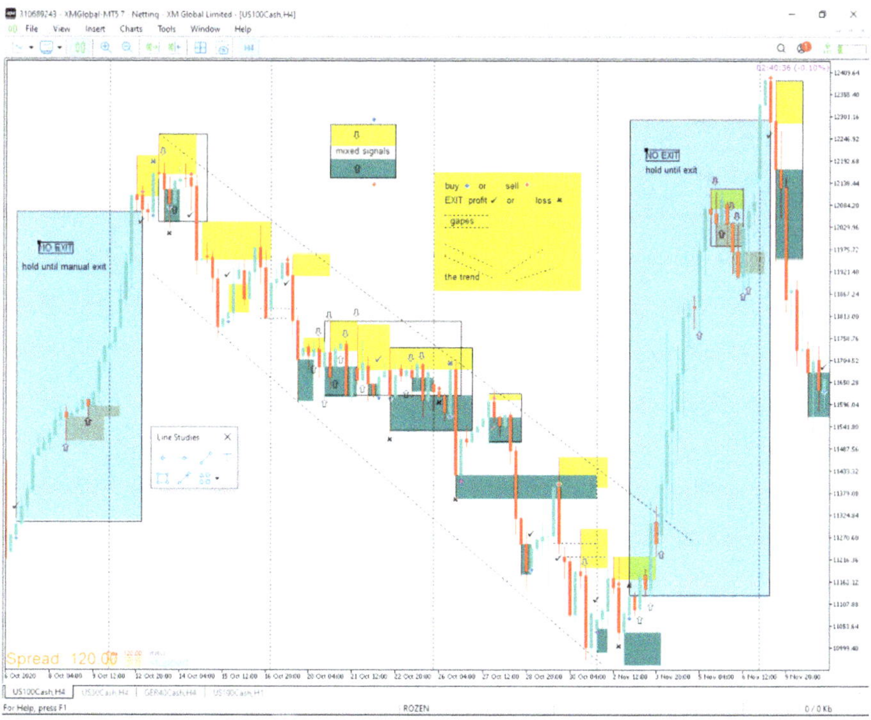

Covering the Gaps

Sometimes, after a strong price movement, the market will leave **gaps**. These are typically visible on the **4-Hour timeframe**. Gaps happen when the price jumps significantly, leaving an empty space on the chart.

If you encounter a gap, don't panic. There's no fixed rule about how the market will behave after a gap, but I want to give you an overview of what to look for in the following images. Understanding how gaps behave can help you make better decisions.

Void Gape Signal (On Period Separation Line)

Weekly gaps should be completely ignored. These gaps can result in **significant losses** or even **blow a small trading account**. Often, they **delay profits** by initially moving against your position before reversing in your favour. Unfortunately, there's **no guaranteed solution** for managing these gaps.

They are also accompanied by **extremely wide spreads** at market open, which increases risk and can lead to unexpected losses. Do **not renter** trades after a gap occurs—simply **avoid trading them altogether**. My best advice: **stay out and ignore weekly gaps** entirely.

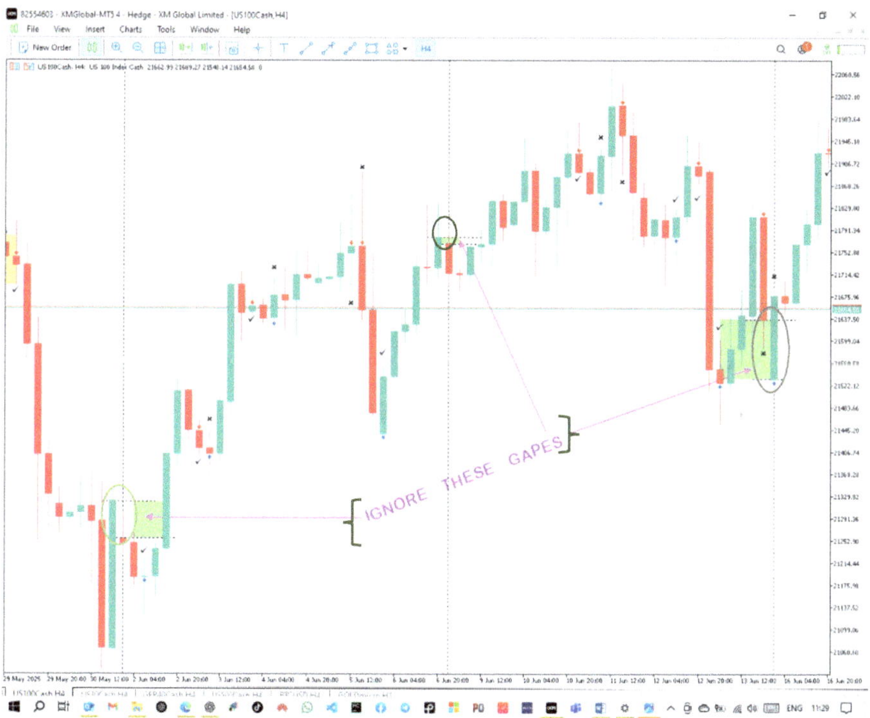

IF ANY VALID SIGNAL APPEAR BEFORE OR AFTER THESE GAPES, PLEASE TAKE THE SIGNAL.

🔹 1. Void Gape Signal (On Period Separation Line)

A **Void Gape** appears **exactly on the period separation line** (typically at weekly open).
These gaps **should be completely ignored** — they carry no meaningful signal and pose significant risk.

! Warning: Weekly gaps often come with **widened spreads** and unpredictable price behavior. They can:

- Blow small accounts,
- Delay profits by moving sharply against your position before reversing,
- Lead to large, unrecoverable losses.

Do **not** re-enter trades once a void gape has occurred.
The best approach? **Avoid trading during weekly opens altogether.**
If a valid signal appears **before or after** a void gape — **only then** consider taking the trade.

GAPES AND SIGNALS – gapes within the period separation

WE HAVE TWO TYPES OF GAPS: ONE THAT OCCURS BEFORE A SIGNAL AND ONE THAT OCCURS AFTER A SIGNAL. THESE GAPS CAN SOMETIMES BE USED AS A TRADING SIGNAL THEMSELVES. HOWEVER, THEY USUALLY OCCUR WITHIN WEEKLY PERIOD SEPARATIONS.

COMING UP NEXT ARE SOME SOLUTIONS TO HANDLE THEM:

Blink Gape Signal **(Immediate After Signal Confirmation)**

A **Blink Gape** occurs **immediately after a confirmed reversal** or **completed base signal** — usually in the same direction as the signal.

⚠ **Important:** This gape should be **completely ignored**.
Simply stick to your original signal entry. Do **not** let the blink confuse you or force early action.
It's just a "flash" — trade the signal, not the blink. If the trade triggers, the gape will affect the future reversal which will be treated as a fake reversal (ghost gape signal).

Ghost Gape Signal **(While a Trade is Active)**

The **Ghost Gape** happens **while a trade is already running (triggered)**.
It usually forms **between two candles moving in the same direction**.

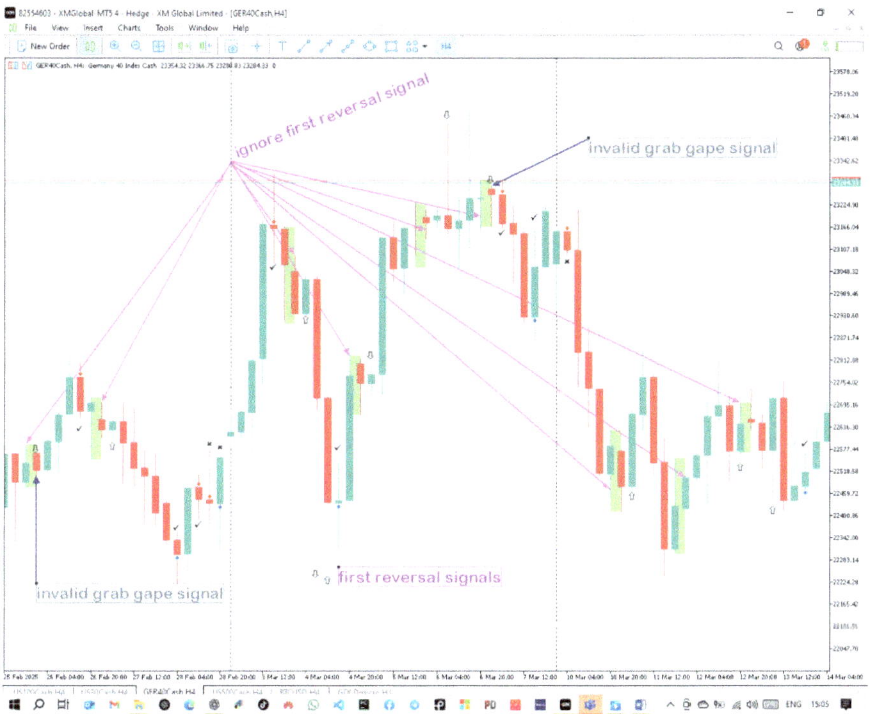

🫣 **Meaning:** This gape is deceptive.
Ignore any reversal signal that appears **immediately after** a ghost gape.
The gap is a ghost — not a valid entry or exit point.

Grab Gape Signal (**Momentum Shift Confirmation**)

🧠 What It Is:

The **Grab Gape** is a **high-probability reversal signal** formed by a gap **between two opposite candles** — one in the direction of the current trend, followed by one with **strong momentum against** that trend.

It's called "Grab" because the market **grabs liquidity**, tricks breakout traders or trend followers — then reverses **hard**.

A **Grab Gape** forms **between two opposite candles**:

- The **first candle** moves in the current trend's direction.
- The **second candle** shows **strong momentum against** the trend — confirming a reversal.

✅ The gape itself is a **signal trigger**, and the **second candle confirms** it.

Entry & SL Rules:

- **Stop Order:** Set **1,200 points** from the second candle.
- The SL must be placed **on the opposite side** of the second candle (above the high for sell, below the low for buy).
- For strong confirmation, the second candle should be **dominant and full-bodied.**

📌 How It Forms (Structure):

1. **First Candle:** Moves **in the direction of the ongoing trend** — often pulls in breakout traders or continues an existing move.
2. **Gap:** Appears between the **close of the first candle** and the **open of the second**. This gap is what **triggers your alert**.
3. **Second Candle:** Reverses **against** the direction of the first, with **strong body and volume**. This confirms the grab —

📊 Signal Logic:

- The first candle **grabs liquidity** — pulling in late buyers or sellers.
- The gap shows **instability** or hidden intention.
- The second candle **violently rejects** the previous move = **confirmation to reverse**.

This is **institutional behavior** — fake move to fill big orders, then sharp reversal.

✅ Entry Rules:

- Enter **at the close of the second candle** (after confirmation).
- Second candle must be:
  - Opposite in direction.
  - Strong-bodied (at least 70–99% or less than 33% full body).
  - Ideally closes beyond the midpoint of the first candle.
- **Watch out for** small doji candles or indecisive second candles.

❌ Invalid If:

- Gap is too small or missing.
- Second candle is weak or indecisive.
- Candle directions are the same.

🛡 Stop Loss & Risk Settings:

- **Default STOP ORDER:** 1,200 points.
- SL is set on the **opposite side of the second candle**:
    - **For a sell:** SL goes **above the high** of the second candle.
    - **For a buy:** SL goes **below the low** of the second candle.
- This SL setup **protects against retests** and **fake outs** (a second trick candle).

🎯 Take Profit Tips:

- Use next major support/resistance **SIGNAL.**
- Trail your SL to new reversal stop order level.

📌 Example Scenarios:

SITUATION	TRADE?	WHY?
1ST CANDLE UP; 2ND CANDLE BIG DOWN	✅ Yes	Perfect grab pattern
1ST CANDLE DOWN, 2ND CANDLE SMALL UP	❌ No	Weak confirmation
1ST AND 2ND CANDLE SAME DIRECTION	❌ No	Not a reversal — ignore
STRONG 2ND CANDLE BUT NO GAP	⚠ Maybe	Watch carefully — not a Grab Gape

---

💬 Final Words:

The **Grab Gape** is **not a basic pattern** — it's a **weapon** when used with discipline.

"Wait for the second candle. The market will show you the trap — then hand you the opportunity."

Engulfing Patterns - Don't Get Emotional

Engulfing patterns can be frustrating, especially when you've held a good trade for hours and then—suddenly—an **opposite candle** comes in and wipes out your profits in a matter of hours. It's natural to feel frustrated, but **revenge trading** is a mistake.

- **Avoid the temptation to shift your stop loss** in an attempt to protect your profits. This is counterproductive.

- Remember: **Don't practice "magic" by trying to manipulate your stops.**

Sometimes, we just need to **wait** for our time to come. The market doesn't owe us anything. **Our time will come**, and when it does, we will achieve great success. Until then, it's about following the strategy and sticking to your plan.

The following are examples of engulfing patterns, the long candles. I have included two candlestick signal patterns:

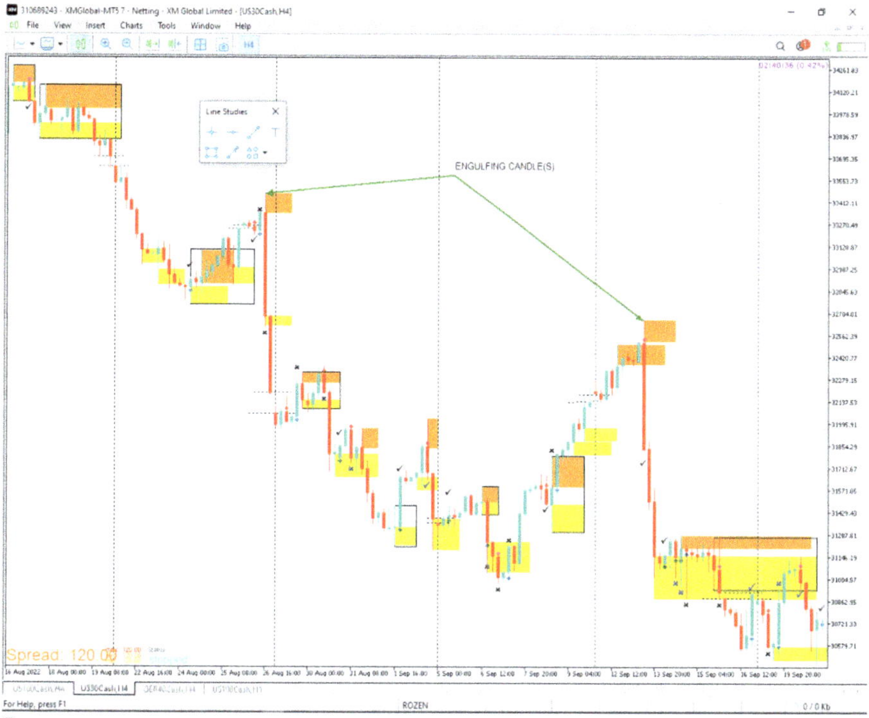
ENGULFING CANDLE(S)

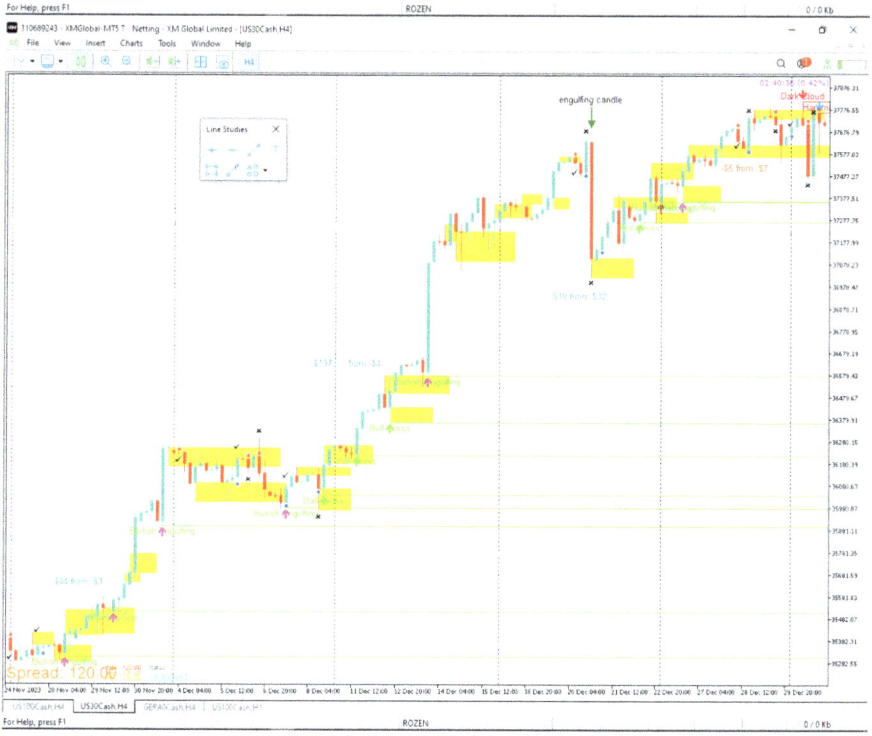
engulfing candle

BS11 → Beast

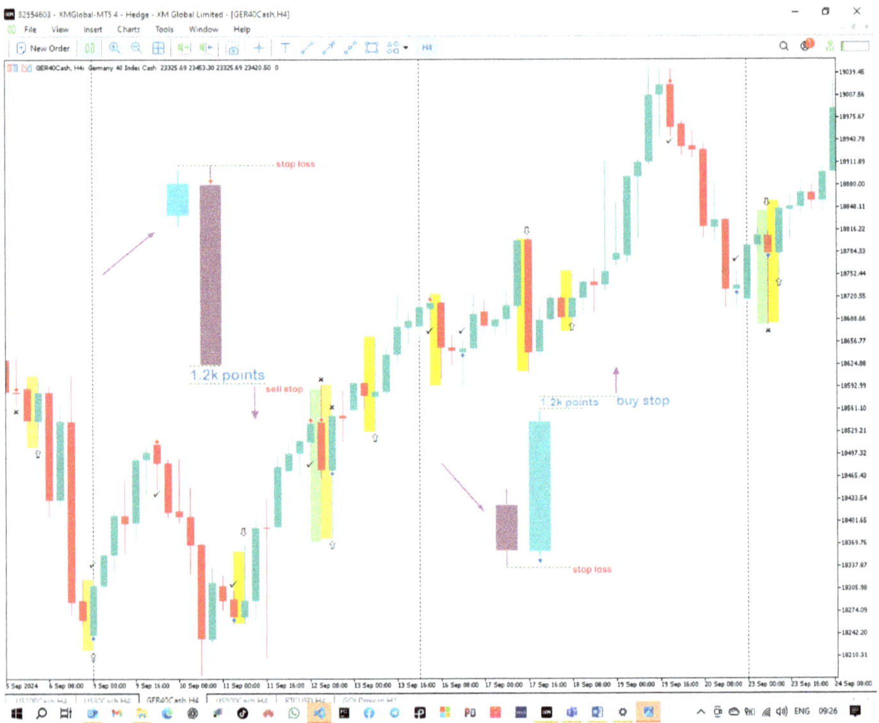

Definition

Base Signal Number eleven is known as **The Beast**. It signals a strong and sudden shift in trend, typically appearing after an extended uptrend (or downtrend for buys). This setup highlights a sharp momentum drop, revealing weakness and offering an unclean entry for reversal trades.

◆ Signal Criteria

SELL Setup:

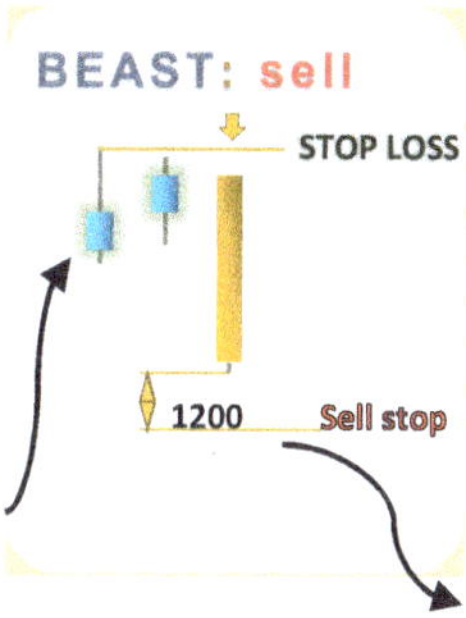

- Market must be coming from an **uptrend**.
- 1 strong **bearish candle** kick off the pattern,
- **Engulfing** 1 or more previous small **bullish** candle(s), contained within the large bearish candle.
- **Entry**: Place a **SELL STOP** 1200 points below the **low of engulfing bearish candle**.
- **Stop Loss**: Set at the open **or high** of the bearish candle.

BUY Setup:

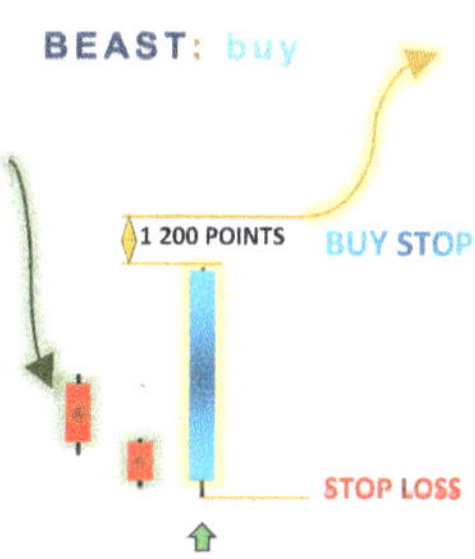

- Market must be coming from a **downtrend**.
- 1 strong bullish candle kick off the pattern.
- **Engulfing** 1 or more previous **small bearish candle(s)**, contained within the large bullish candle.
- **Entry**: Place a **BUY STOP** 1200 points above the **high of the engulfing bullish candle**.
- **Stop Loss**: Set at the open or low of the first bullish candle.

◈ Weak Signals

- The engulfing candles is not aggressive or large-bodied.
- Occurs in sideways markets without a prior strong trend.

◆ Entry & Stop Loss Strategy

- **Use stop orders only.**
- Entry: 1200 points beyond the engulfing candle.
- SL: Set at the open of the engulfing candle.
- Cancel the order if not triggered within 4 hours.

◈ Conditions to Confirm the Signal

- Appears after a clean trend move (uptrend for sells, downtrend for buys).
- Clear imbalance and strong momentum shift in the engulfing candle.

◈ Invalid Signals

- Engulfing candle doesn't engulf or show a strong momentum shift.
- Engulfing candle appears after a FVG or gapes in 4-Hour time frame.
- Candle appears during ranging market.

◈ Order Management

- If entry doesn't trigger within 4hours, cancel and wait for a new setup.

TURN OVER

BS12 → The Fall

Definition

Base Signal Number Eleven is known as **The Fall**. It signals a strong and sudden shift in trend, typically appearing after an extended uptrend (or downtrend for buys). This setup highlights a sharp momentum drop followed by a failed recovery attempt, revealing weakness and offering a clean entry for reversal trades.

◈ Signal Logic

The pattern plays out in three main phases:

1. **Phase ① – The Drop:**
    - One or two large **bearish candles** (or **bullish for buys**) that mark an aggressive shift in market sentiment.
    - This initiates the structure and creates a dominant range.
2. **Phase ② – The Reaction:**
    - One or two **small candles** (typically bullish if selling, bearish if buying) that form **inside** the range of Phase ①.
    - These show a weak attempt at a pullback or consolidation, trapped within the earlier aggression.
3. **Phase ③ – The Confirmation:**
    - A single **neutral or weak candle**, often with a small body or dominant wick, still **inside the range** of the first one or two bearish candles.
    - This final candle confirms the failure of the pullback and sets up the entry.

◆ Signal Criteria

SELL Setup:

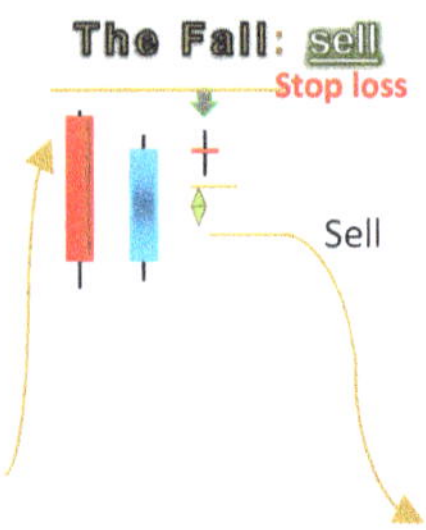

- Market must be coming from an **uptrend**.
- 1–2 strong **bearish candles** kick off the pattern.
- Followed by 1–2 **small bullish candles**, contained inside the body of the large bearish candle(s).
- Final confirmation is a **small bearish or neutral candle**, still inside the original bearish candle's body.
- **Entry**: Place a **SELL STOP** 1200 points below the **low of the third candle**.
- **Stop Loss:** Set at any **high**, **open** **or** **close** of any candle in the three phases.

BUY Setup:

Market must be coming from a **downtrend**.

1–2 strong **bullish candles** kick off the pattern.

Followed by 1–2 **small bearish candles**, contained within the large bullish candle(s).

Final confirmation is a **small bullish or neutral candle**, still inside the initial bullish candle's body.

Entry: Place a **BUY STOP** 1200 points above the **high of the third candle**.

Stop Loss: Set at any **high**, **open** **or** **close** of any candle in the three phases.

◈ Weak Signals

- The first 1–2 candles are not aggressive or large-bodied.
- The small candles in Phase ② are too strong or break the range of Phase ①.
- The confirming candle (Phase ③) closes outside the initial large candle range.
- Occurs in sideways markets without a prior strong trend.

◆ Entry & Stop Loss Strategy

- **Use stop orders only.**
- Entry: 1200 points beyond the confirming candle (candle ③).
- SL: Varies, use any of the candle in phase one, two or three.
- Cancel the order if not triggered within 4 hours.

◆ Conditions to Confirm the Signal

- Appears after a clean trend move (uptrend for sells, downtrend for buys).
- Clear imbalance and strong momentum shift in the first 1–2 candles.
- The final candle stays inside the range of the initiating candle(s).
- Weak or trapped reaction candles indicate failed counter pressure.

◆ Invalid Signals

- Confirming candle closes outside the range of the initiating candles.
- Pullback candles (middle phase) show strength or attempt breakouts.
- SL area does not protect against a meaningful invalidation point.

◆ Order Management

If entry doesn't trigger within 4hours, cancel and wait for a new setup.

Summary

- **Major vs. Minor Signals**: Always distinguish between the two and wait for confirmation before acting.
- **Long Wicks & Stop Hunts**: Be aware of sudden market movements that can hit your stops and mislead your trade.
- **Trend Patience**: Wait for confirmation of the trend before acting, and be patient in your approach.
- **Covering the Gaps**: Gaps can occur, and understanding how to navigate them will help you manage risk.
- **Engulfing Patterns**: Don't let emotional reactions lead you to make rash decisions. Stick to your strategy.

The images I've provided will give you a better understanding of these concepts. **Stay calm, stick to your plan, and remember that every trade is a step in your journey**. Trust the process and **focus on the long-term results**.

Phase Eleven: Capital and Multiplication

No One is Coming to Save You – Save Yourself

This is no time to wait for a savior. You've been waiting long enough. **Not everything in the store is for sale**, and there's a **cheaper store** where **Peter Panther** and I shop.

You are **not a lost boy**. You are good enough as you are. The reason you feel stuck is because you've been lied to. You've been told that you need to depend on money, but **money serves you**, not the other way around. You are the **creator**, and money is your creation. Without you, there is no money.

Money is everywhere, just like everything else you need. You were born with nothing, but now you have clothes, you speak, and you do things. **Having nothing is not the end of the world**, but rather the beginning of your world. **Having everything is the end of it**.

You will **speak money** like your own language. **It's your turn. Your beginning is now.**

How to Get Lucky

The foundation of this world was never built on money. Money isn't running the world—**faith doesn't work** in the way you think. The only thing that truly works is **action**.

You only get lucky when you take **action**. It doesn't matter if you're not prepared—**time waits for no one**. In five years, you'll be older, and time will have run out. It's okay to take risks in pursuing something meaningful while you still can, because **you can't wait forever**.

Bootstrapping Your Journey

If you don't have enough capital to start a business, **you can start as a salesperson** and save money to fund your own venture. The same applies to **forex trading**. If you don't have enough to start trading, you could start a small business and save money to invest in trading later.

Remember, **money is everywhere**. Every town you see today was once an empty land—someone did something about it, and so can you. **You don't have to start with what you love.** You can get a job and save until you have enough to invest. Once you have the capital, you can decide to destroy what you don't like and move on.

Getting an Investor

You don't need your own money to start trading—what you need is an investor. Master the strategy first, then seek out an investor.

Important Tips:

- Do not sabotage your investor.
- Create a contract that ensures **your independence**.
- Don't rush things—take your time.
- Don't ask for a large amount of capital—start small.

Getting a client

There are many people who know about forex but don't know how to trade. It's okay to trade for them or provide signals and receive payment in return. However, **don't lie to your clients**. Only promise what you can deliver.

You should also complete the manual and tests provided to ensure you know how to trade before offering your services.

Starting a Rizen Forex Community (RFxC)

Maybe you don't have enough capital to trade alone, but you know someone who's also interested in trading. **Join forces**—combine your resources to open a joint account. You can trade with a team of up to 10 people and **share the profits** until you all have enough capital to trade individually.

The Power of Lot Size vs. Greed

Greed is a part of every trader's life, whether positive or negative. It's not something you can easily escape; it's a result of **psychological reasons**. The key is to **channel greed positively**—don't let it control you.

I wrote this book when I had nothing. **If I were already rich**, I would have never gained the power that comes from struggling and growing. Sometimes, the desire for more pushes you to take action. But **don't let greed make you do reckless things**.

Greedy 01: Perfect vs. Imperfect Signals

Time is short, and you may feel overwhelmed by your situation. You might be tempted to trade recklessly, but **take your time**. Start with a small amount—say, **$20**—and risk it by trading carefully using leverage (like 1:1000) to build your equity. The goal is to take only **perfect signals**. If you lose everything, that's okay—it's part of the process.

Greedy 02: Multiplying vs. Gambling

If you've been trading for a while and find yourself blowing your accounts, don't worry. You are not alone.

Here's my plan for you:

1. **Use the money you're willing to lose** to test out trading strategies.
2. Stick to **perfect signals** and trade **one index** at a time.
3. **Start a new account** to trade without breaking your trading rules.
4. Protect your main account and treat it with respect.

You might lose everything, or you might get lucky and multiply your account. **It's all part of the journey.**

Final Thoughts

Don't wait for someone to save you. Take action. **You are the creator**, and you must shape your own future. Whether you start small or with an investor, the key is **doing something**—you'll never succeed by doing nothing. Take risks, follow your strategy, and **believe in yourself**. Your time is now.

Conclusion

No one's coming. No secret mentor. No holy signal. Just you.

The power? It's always been yours. But power means nothing without control.
Growth isn't pretty—it breaks you. You'll lose comfort. You'll bury old versions of yourself. And that's the cost. That's the price of levelling up.

I've lost more times than I can count. But each loss carved away what I didn't need. That's how you build clarity—from chaos.

The Queen was never the goal. The King is. Your core.
Your discipline.
Your peace.
Protect that.

Belief isn't inherited—it's built. Alone. At 3 a.m. In silence.
No applause. No shortcut. Just you, the screen, and the decision to stay sharp.

You made it this far.
You've seen the system. You've felt the shift.

Now finish the game.
Grow the tree.
Print the money.

You know what to do.

www.ingramcontent.com/pod-product-compliance
Lightning Source LLC
LaVergne TN
LVHW022219200926
848481LV00006B/2034
* 9 7 8 1 0 3 7 0 9 5 6 3 4 *